The Entrepreneur's Guide to Raising Capital

Recent Titles in
The Entrepreneur's Guide

The Entrepreneur's Guide to Managing Growth and Handling Crises
Theo J. van Dijk

The Entrepreneur's Guide to Writing Business Plans and Proposals
K. Dennis Chambers

The Entrepreneur's Guide to Hiring and Building the Team
Ken Tanner

The Entrepreneur's Guide to Managing Information Technology
CJ Rhoads

The Entrepreneur's Guide to Successful Leadership
Dan Goldberg and Don Martin

The Entrepreneur's Guide to Marketing
Robert F. Everett

The Entrepreneur's Guide

CJ Rhoads, Series Editor

The Entrepreneur's Guide to Raising Capital

David Nour

Westport, Connecticut
London

Library of Congress Cataloging-in-Publication Data

Nour, David, 1968
   The Entrepreneur's guide to raising capital / David Nour.
     p. cm.—(The entrepreneur's guide, ISSN 1939–2478)
   Includes bibliographical references and index.
   ISBN 978–0–313–35602–5 (alk. paper)
   1. New business enterprises—Finance. 2. Small business—Finance.
   3. Venture capital. I. Title.
   HG4027.6.N68   2009
   658.15′224—dc22   2008047579

British Library Cataloguing in Publication Data is available.

Library of Congress Catalog Card Number: 2008047579
ISBN: 978–0–313–35602–5
ISSN: 1939–2478

First published in 2009

Praeger Publishers, 88 Post Road West, Westport, CT 06881
An imprint of Greenwood Publishing Group, Inc.
www.praeger.com

Printed in the United States of America

∞

The paper used in this book complies with the
Permanent Paper Standard issued by the National
Information Standards Organization (Z39.48–1984).

10 9 8 7 6 5 4 3 2 1

Contents

Acknowledgments   vii

Introduction   ix

1. Why Undercapitalized Companies Don't Survive   1

2. Smart Capital   14

3. Plan Now or Pay Later   23

4. Bootstrapping and Early-Stage Creative Capital   33

5. Big Guns: Institutional Investors   50

6. Avenues for Alternative Capital   74

7. IPOs, Reverse Mergers, and International Markets   82

8. Valuations, Acquisitions, and Exit Strategies   95

9. Value-Added Financial Intermediaries   112

10. The Experts Speak: Best Practices to Embrace and Top Mistakes to Avoid   125

Appendixes   137

    A: The Ultimate Resource Library   137

    B: Google's S-1 Filing   168

Index   181

Acknowledgments

This project would not have been possible without the candid input of entrepreneurs, investment intermediary professionals, and investors alike. Their entrepreneurial resilience and sheer will to adapt to market dynamics is inspiring; their collective content, expertise, and experiential knowledge pave the road for others to follow.

In my personal journey to raise capital, I owe a great deal of gratitude to former CEOs, including Bruce Kasanoff, Christian Gheorghe, and Rick Brennan; to venture capital and private equity partners such as Erik Jansen, Tim Connor, and John Patton; and to professional service providers such as Dom Mazzone, Kent Webb, and John Hurley. Over the past three decades, they, along with countless others, have provided invaluable insights into my personal development and professional efforts.

My thanks go to series editor C. J. Rhoads, Jeff Olson, and their teams at Praeger/ABC-CLIO for supporting this endeavor.

Finally, I dedicate this book to Wendy, Grayson, and Justus. Without your unconditional love and support, my passion for learning, writing, and growing through these projects would not be possible. You are the love of my life.

Introduction

- "You're too early for us."
- "You're too late for us."
- "Get a lead investor and then we'll join."
- "We don't have experience in your industry."
- "We have a conflict of interest."
- "I liked your deal, but my partners didn't."
- "You need to prove that this business can scale."
- "The timing isn't good for us in the current economy."
- "The geography isn't ideal."

Everything is a challenge in the life of an entrepreneur, and raising capital is no exception. Stick around the fundraising business long enough, and you'll hear every response imaginable to your plea for money.

Over the last several years, in interviewing more than a thousand entrepreneurs of early-stage, growth-oriented ventures—including both those that were and those that were not externally funded—all have concurred, without exception, that raising capital was one of their toughest challenges. It's time consuming, it's distracting from the core competency of the business, and—if no one else tells you, let me—it's a huge pain.

At times, you'll feel belittled by gatekeepers who just learned how to shave last week, and insulted by those who know a fraction of what you know (since, after all, you've researched and survived getting the business to where it is today). You'll be questioned about your ideas, your vision, and the future viability of the business with you at the helm. But if you can get through the maze, if you can understand the broad sources of available capital, if you can survive the beauty contests of those who judge the quality of the deal—all while making a stand for the business you have built—the capital you receive can become the fuel for making your vision a reality.

WHY YOU SHOULD READ THIS BOOK

This book is a how-to guide designed to help entrepreneurs navigate the capital-raising labyrinth, answering the most common, yet often perplexing, questions:

- How do I realize the promised benefits of raising outside capital?
- How do I avoid the risks associated with various sources of capital?
- How do I plan for the right type, amount, and source of capital as the business evolves in its natural lifecycle?
- How do I avoid diluting my credibility with current and prospective investors?
- How do I choose wisely from the plethora of financial and strategic investors, consultants, merchant bankers, and middlemen?
- How do I avoid wasting precious capital that won't help me move the business forward?
- How do I get the most out of every dollar of outside capital I raise?

Beyond my passion for helping intelligent and engaging entrepreneurs succeed, my goal in this book is to provide real-life, practical, pragmatic advice from other entrepreneurs who have struggled with the same set of challenges. In the process, I hope to help you realize that, whether you're operating a growing business or a mature one, being an entrepreneur is all about doing what others tell you is impossible to accomplish.

In the coming chapters, I'll cover the fundamental challenges of operating a cash-poor or highly undercapitalized business. I'll discuss the very real difference between smart and dumb capital raises, and the need for astute strategic financial planning. And I'll review the different types of capital—from bootstrapping and creative financing such as factoring or licensing, to angels and the more mature market of institutional investors.

By understanding what venture capital and private equity firms look for, you can begin to position your business as an attractive investment opportunity. For those who have aspirations of going to the public market, I'll cover initial public offerings (IPOs), reverse mergers, and raising capital through international markets. One of the bigger challenges will be navigating your way through this process, so I'll cover the plethora of intermediaries such as investment or merchant bankers and mergers-and-acquisitions experts. I'll also talk about valuations and strategic alliances, and finally I'll wrap up with the top mistakes many make in the process and provide the ultimate resource guide to places, organizations, and publications.

1

Why Undercapitalized Companies Don't Survive

How do you define wealth? My friend and mentor, Alan Weiss, defines it as "discretionary time"! He says we can always make more money, but we'll never be able to create more time.

BUILDING WEALTH

Why did you become an entrepreneur? Was it the perceived freedom in lifestyle, the financial security, or simply because you knew how to do the job better than many of those who previously hired you? Did you identify a market niche that you thought you could exploit, or did you finally amass enough broad-based expertise to justify the risk of going out on your own? There are a number of great books that dive into the psychology, challenges, and opportunities of entrepreneurs in the market today—from the other books in *The Entrepreneur's Guide* series, to *The E-Myth Revisited* (1995) by Michael Gerber, to *The Art of the Start* (2004) by Guy Kawasaki.

Money gives us the freedom to do what we want, when we want, and with whom we want. In every business, the money needed to buy equipment, develop a product or service, expand a product line or geographic location, or hire more sales or marketing resources can be perceived as a necessary evil. With expansion and scale, what you own can often lead to owning you!

Capital is defined as the financial resources (cash, debt, leasing, equity, and so forth) that help a business survive and grow. Many companies are either unwilling or unable to invest the appropriate resources to enlarge their business, whether by growing their market share; expanding their products and services, marketing, or advertising campaigns to win more business; or simply adding or developing their people to deliver more sales or better customer service. With limited or no access to capital, your ability to grow will be handicapped. Add market dynamics into the equation—such as competitors, new technological tools (what did we all do before BlackBerry or Google searches?), and the growing demands of your current and prospective clients, not to mention challenging economic conditions—and it's easy to see why status quo simply will not suffice.

WHAT IS RAISING CAPITAL ALL ABOUT?

Before you get started, it is critical first to understand that raising capital is not just about the money. It's often about attracting, retaining, and deepening a relationship with a financial or strategic partner, who develops a vested interest in the long-term viability and success of the business.

Let me say that again: Successful fundraising is about attracting, retaining, and deepening a candid, mutually respectful, and trustworthy relationship with an appropriate financial partner at the right stage in your business's life cycle. As the business matures through a natural evolution, it requires distinctly unique amounts and types of capital, which often dictate possible primary and secondary sources. Access to these sources becomes a challenge, as many investors seldom accept "cold calls" or unsolicited offerings.

Over the past decade, I have reviewed hundreds of business plans, sat in on countless board meetings, and reviewed everything from outrageous "land-grab" opportunities to yet another online pet or furniture store. I've lived through the wishful thinking and half-truths entrepreneurs espouse when they're trying to raise capital, and I've heard what investors say to entrepreneurs' faces and what they say after they leave.

The common denominator among those who are successful in raising capital has always been not only the entrepreneurs' practical, pragmatic, and well-researched market opportunity but also their ability to articulate a believable vision and, much more importantly, to execute the economic fundamentals. With execution, performance, and results comes credibility, believability, and trust—trust that encourages funders to invest initially and to continue to reinvest, as well as to introduce entrepreneurs to other people who can help the venture reduce risk and accelerate profitable growth.

Exercise 1.1
Intended Use of Capital

Candidly list your top five intended uses for capital and the desired outcome from each.

	Intended Use of Capital	*Desired Outcome*
1.		
2.		
3.		
4.		
5.		

INDUSTRY NUANCES

Most astute investors tend to bet on the jockey and not the horse. That is not to say they know any less about the horse, though. They know the horse's required training regimen and the ground conditions on which the jockey will ride that horse, hopefully to a strong finish. But because they know the horse so well, they develop a knack for identifying critical traits in jockeys that will get the absolute most out of the horse. They also recognize the right supporting team the horse and jockey will need to manage their performance over time, and the appropriate course corrections that might need to be made—including replacing the jockey, if necessary—along the way.

That's why savvy investors tend to focus on a particular industry. Either through their own personal and professional experience—such as being a banker for thirty-plus years—or by having made several investments in the particular industry, they understand that industry's nuances well. For example, they might intuitively understand the challenges faced in the restaurant industry: its capital-intensive nature, its unpredictable workforce, and the economic effects of modern-day fads. Or perhaps they know the retail industry, with its strict inventory and distribution requirements, teenage and often financially fickle workforce, and real estate and merchandising requirements.

These investors recognize that, in the professional services industry, the most valuable assets are the people traveling up and down office elevators every day. Without a repeatable, predictable method and recurring revenue stream from long-term contracts, consistent profit is difficult to determine. And they know all too well that an interesting idea may make a product, but an interesting product does not make a company!

On the positive side, they also understand the power and potential of unique concepts in an age-old industry. Take Chipotle Mexican Grill, for example. It started with founder and CEO Steve Ells's vision in 1993 when he opened the doors of the first Chipotle restaurant near the University of Denver. Ells wanted to use his skills as a chef to make great-tasting burritos and tacos for the public. His vision was simple: Provide fresh, reasonably priced food, served in a casual and hip atmosphere.

Although Ells's concept was fairly straightforward, many of his early investors saw it as a unique approach to a very crowded, often highly segmented market. (The options at the time were typically no-taste fast food joints or individual, authentic, mom-and-pop-owned local outlets.) Today, through its Food with Integrity mission, Chipotle buys the highest-quality ingredients from the highest-quality sources and has trained its staff to make customers' favorite burritos or tacos, with the very best ingredients, right in front of them. With hundreds of restaurants across the country now, Chipotle is a solid example of a unique concept that an entrepreneur was able to position to investors as something they could believe in.

Exercise 1.2
Industry Nuances and Unique Approaches

What are the top three industry nuances that an objective investor could consider to be a hindrance to the success of your business? What are your direct responses or unique approach to addressing each? Try listing them here.

Industry Nuance/Hindrance	*Direct Response/Unique Approach*
1.	
2.	
3.	

WEATHERING BROADER ECONOMIC CONDITIONS

Undercapitalized companies simply won't thrive or even survive for long. According to Adam Ogburn, corporate banking manager and senior vice president of Georgian Bank: "It is really difficult for a company that's undercapitalized to weather varying economic conditions. When the market is strong, you lack the capital to invest, grow, and take advantage of the opportunities. And if you are undercapitalized, when the market turns down, you are generally in trouble because you don't have the wherewithal to get through those tough times."

Founded in 2002, Georgian Bank has $2 billion in assets and focuses on corporate and private banking. Adam serves a focused market of middle-size companies in corporate banking—companies with revenues of $50 million to $150 million—looking to finance acquisitions, growth capital, and real estate purchases. Adam looks for company profiles that generally include solid financial performance for at least three years, rapid growth, and solid equity built during the economic boom with their profitability and steady expansion.

Growth in these types of companies often requires expanded accounts receivable and inventory, utilizing cash and thus creating a need for working capital in $1 million to $20 million loans to continue their evolutionary development. Generally, if a company is growing rapidly but doesn't seek out sufficient capital to support that growth, it can put its survival at risk.

Many companies may be able to generate enough revenue to cover their expenses, but to become stronger competitors and ideally dominate their niche, territory, or particular focus, they must invest significant capital. Given the competitive nature of the market, the one that gets there first is not necessarily the one with the best offering.

Rusty Gordon should know. He is the former CEO of Knowlagent, a leading software-as-a-service (SaaS) company that trains and manages call-center agents so that they can provide superior sales and customer service. Over the years and through economic booms and busts, Rusty has raised some twenty rounds of financing for five or six different companies—an estimated $75 million.

"I think undercapitalized companies are at a real risk—especially in a turbulent economy," Rusty says. "A lot of software companies are now transforming their traditional enterprise software development, sales, and service model to one of software-as-a-service model, which takes more initial capitalization to launch successfully and gain market traction."

How much risk is involved? It depends on when the financing occurs in their cycle. Rusty and many other high-tech CEOs believe that companies that are just getting a real foothold in the market and are undercapitalized can lose what is often their only market opportunity. "The market is getting smarter about when to fund," he says, "so there are a lot of companies that are funded relatively heavily in the beginning right after their angel round, and then they can't effectively use the money."

Exercise 1.3
Economic Conditions and Your Options

What five broad economic conditions could have an adverse effect on your ability to perform, execute, or deliver results—for example, what if that big customer takes three months to pay your last invoice or that critical supplier goes out of business? What if the turbulent economy remains in a recession for a long period of time? List your proactive options to address each condition.

Detrimental Economic Conditions ("*What could uniquely hurt us?*")	*Proactive Options* ("*What can we do about it now?*")
1.	
2.	
3.	
4.	
5.	

BEYOND THE CHASM

In his groundbreaking work *Crossing the Chasm: Marketing and Selling High-Tech Products to Mainstream Customers* (1999), Geoffrey Moore illustrated the technology adoption life cycle (see figure 1.1). Moore segmented technology buyers into five groups: Innovators, Early Adopters, Early Majority, Late Majority, and Laggards. Each group represents psychographic profiles with unique marketing response profiles. In 1991, Moore wrote, "To cross the chasm you must target a market segment defined around a must-have value proposition."

The same market segmentation of technology companies and buyers that Moore applied in his chasm discussion can be applied to entrepreneurs and investors in various industries. Each investor puts money in a company based on a set of parameters: risk tolerances, an acceptable range of investment criteria (such as the amount of investment required over some period

Figure 1.1
Geoffrey Moore's Technology Adoption Life Cycle

Innovators	Early Adopters	Early Majority	Late Majority	Laggards

Risk Adverse

Open Minded

More Skeptical

Less Price Sensitive

Chasm

Source: Adapted from *Crossing the Chasm* (HarperBusiness, 1999).

of time), and pre- and post-investment valuation (the value of the investment, as covered in chapter 8—similar to the appraisal of a house compared to others in the neighborhood). These parameters have a range, depending on the investor's perception of a business and the market it serves.

Are you creating a new market with your innovation such that the target buyer has to be "educated" on how to use it for the desired benefit? If so, this approach will take longer to create awareness and acceptance (read: considerably more capital). Or, on the other hand, are you building a better mousetrap—improving an existing process or product that target buyers can easily understand and begin to apply to the challenges or opportunities they face in their own businesses or lives? How you position your business *today* versus the future will heavily depend on both your due diligence and your articulation of the current and anticipated financial requirements of the business.

Depending on the business you are running, you may need significant money early in the business life cycle to develop and test a new product or service. With a handful of customers, you may be able to prove the value of your solution, but then you need additional capital to take your product or services beyond the early customers to the mainstream. If you continue to grow and perhaps need capital for strategic alliances, international expansion, or buying other businesses, your business may need to be repositioned to bigger investors.

Notes Rusty Gordon of Knowlagent: "In our background, there was a technology change—the Internet and transition to SaaS—which is another funding need. There is also another level of need for additional capital—when you begin to build the business beyond what you can grow it organically, you begin to look for mergers and acquisitions."

Exercise 1.4
Target Market, Buyers, and Focused Solutions

Where is your target focus on the "chasm" bell curve? Can you succinctly define your Ideal Customer Profile (ICP) or Ideal Buyer Profile (IBP) that may have the challenges you are trying to solve? How do you know? Take a minute to capture your thoughts:

A. Our products and services (holistically) serve the _____
[choose one of the profiles in figure 1.1] category. We know this because [provide some validation such as majority of current customers or buyers and their attitudes]:

_____
_____
_____
_____

B. Our ideal customer/buyer profile is [describe what type of company or individual buyer has the exact challenges your product or service addresses]:

_____
_____
_____
_____
_____

KNOWING WHEN TO START AND FROM WHERE TO GET THE MONEY

A big mistake many first-time fundraising entrepreneurs make is that they raise too little money and start the process entirely too late. Fundamentally, when your business is in the midst of rapid growth, it is an incredibly inconvenient time to be constrained by going broke!

"I recommend that companies start six to nine months earlier than they think they should and raise more than they think they should," says Cate Cavanagh Krensavage, managing partner of Palo Alto Capital Partners, a boutique investment bank that specializes in private placements for small companies.

Cate and her team focus on early stage financing for private companies and are typically a smaller participant. According to her, entrepreneurs generally plan to raise enough capital for two years, but in more recent turbulent economic climates, they should be planning for a three- to five-year period instead.

"If you don't have the working capital for growth—apart from missing your numbers, which investors don't like—you are also missing your opportunity in the market," she says. "If you don't have enough money to invest in your development or execution of your plan to hit your sales numbers, you will give direct competitors time to catch up. Before you know it, someone who was way behind you is now way ahead because they were able to continue raising capital to execute their plan."

Another challenge you should consider is the amount and source of the capital. You want to raise the smallest amount of money to meet your next financial milestones so that you can raise money later at a higher valuation.

That's one trajectory. The other is: "When the cookies are being handed out, you take as many cookies as you possibly can," in the words of Larry Bock, special limited partner at Lux Capital, where he currently serves as chairman of the Lux Ventures advisory board, a collection of industry experts advising the firm's investment team. He adds, "The kinds of companies that I get involved in, which are broad-based platform technology companies, I'm always one who thinks you should raise as much money as you can."

INVESTMENT ELASTICITY: SUFFICIENT INTEREST AND DEEP ENOUGH POCKETS FOR FUTURE ROUNDS

Larry Bock was, by far, one of the most direct entrepreneurs I interviewed. Having experienced the fundraising process several times through high-quality institutional investors (see chapter 5 on "big guns"), he reiterated the critical nature of raising capital from appropriate sources—those who are willing and able to invest in your type of business or industry and who have direct and relevant experience with the financing challenges and opportunities ahead from their past investment experiences. Larry drove the point home that these investors need to remain sufficiently interested

Exercise 1.5
Timing, Amount, and Sources of Your Fundraising

When should you start looking to raise capital, how much should you go for, and from what appropriate sources? It's critical to begin thinking about these three points very early in the process. Even if you don't have sufficient background information right now, start forming some critical early assumptions to build your efforts around.

Step 1. Begin with the end goal in mind. If you want access to the funds to begin investing for the critical purposes you outlined in exercise 1.1, circle the date you need the money and map out your strategy six to nine months in advance. Write that date here: _____

Step 2. How much capital do you believe you need? _____

How did you come up with this figure?

_____

_____

_____

Step 3. What are your current top three targets to investigate as potential sources of capital?

1. _____
2. _____
3. _____

---

not only in you as the entrepreneur but also in your vision for the idea and the evolution of the company during the entire life cycle of the business.

"If I know I'm going to have to raise $100 million in order to get the technology commercialized over the next five to ten years, for example, it doesn't make any sense for me to go after angel investors (who may typically invest $1 million and look to exit in one or two years)," he explains. "I'm going to want a broad base of institutional investors involved early on—and the high-quality ones—so that future rounds are made very easily and I can focus on running the business." Sources who can put in multiple rounds of financing and have the ability to invest over the life span of the company can help entrepreneurs reach the performance results they are after.

MANAGEMENT BENCH STRENGTH

Another interesting perspective on this topic of undercapitalized companies being able to survive and thrive in the long term comes from André Schnabl, managing partner of the Atlanta office of Grant Thornton LLP a national accounting and business services firm that provides an array of services including audit, tax, and business advisory services to entrepreneurial and public company clients. "I think it has to do with how you approach the issue of undercapitalization," says André. "Beyond what industry the company is in, we consider: What created the condition? What strategic conditions will create survival and make it thrive? There are a broad range of other issues, but the most important is temperament and breadth of management."

According to André, companies with a weak balance sheet are at a clear competitive disadvantage. This is apparent as more and more private equity groups inflate balance sheets in order to maximize the internal rate of return (IRR) for their limited partner investors. In the meantime, they put their portfolio companies at a disadvantage. This is in stark contrast to the well-capitalized entrepreneurial or family-owned businesses chasing the exact same market.

Critical Definitions

Private equity group (PEG)	Professional investors managing a pool of capital who invest in private companies or real property, often purchasing a majority controlling interest in operating companies or commercial real estate projects.
Inflated balance sheet	A balance sheet in which a more favorable financial position of the company is reflected by reporting higher cash assets or lower cost bases (the original costs of assets) or by presenting operating costs as investments.

(continued)

Internal rate of return (IRR)	The interest rate investors look for in their investments, minus the cost of investing that capital.
Premoney valuation	The value of a company before an investor's money is invested.
Postmoney valuation	The value of a company after an investor's money is invested, equal to the premoney valuation plus the investment.

Beyond the founder, many investors focus on the "bench strength" of the management team and prefer to work with companies whose needs can be met by the skills and guidance that the particular investor possesses. In this case, rather than differentiating or targeting companies of a particular size, it becomes more a function of what the companies' need is and the character and health of the company—matched with the investors' breadth and depth of insights and resources.

Exercise 1.6
Critical Bench Strength Areas

There are five critical areas where an entrepreneur typically needs bench strength:

1. CEO—vision, mission, chief advocate
2. Sales—all about revenue and customers
3. Marketing—market positioning, awareness, lead generation
4. Product Development—make it, deliver it, enhance it
5. Operations—finance/admin/legal

Who is your go-to team? (By the way, given our "free-agent nation," it's okay to outsource some of the noncore functions.)

_____
_____
_____

Are your (internal or external) resources battle-tested to consistently deliver on commitments made? Would they pass an independent investor's due-diligence research in terms of a proven, relevant track record?

_____
_____
_____

It's okay not to have all the boxes in an org chart filled in, but it's *not* okay not to have thought about this in depth before you walk into an investor's office!

_____
_____
_____
_____
_____

UNDERCAPITALIZED FRUGALNESS

If there is a positive aspect of being undercapitalized, one could argue it is that of forcing frugality on the CEO. Several serial entrepreneurs I interviewed believe that externally funded, early-stage companies spend much more money than necessary. When asked about the causal factors of this phenomenon, three explanations were consistently offered:

- Lack of required expertise: They simply didn't know what they didn't know and they spent way too much money trying to learn or acquire the necessary expertise in a particular area.
- Ignorance of the marketplace or bad counsel: It is critical to intimately understand the dynamics or nuances of your market; bad advice regarding a flawed strategy or inept execution in your target market can be very expensive.
- Misplaced comfort level regarding a recent capital raise: Because it is "someone else's money," you get a false sense of security by having that money in your account to spend. What many entrepreneurs don't understand is that they are stewards of that resource and need to carefully and accurately evaluate where and how they spend it—every dollar matters!

Alec Peters, CEO of ScreamingSports.com, a technology company in the fantasy sports world, is one such critic. Alec began his career in sports marketing, coached volleyball at the University of Southern California, and created Auctionworks, eBay's number-one partner for sales automation. Says Alec, "If I was to start Auctionworks now—we raised $5 million and spent it basically in the first four years of the company—I believe we could do it all over again and accomplish the same thing with $2 million."

When asked if managing a tight budget can be a blessing, Alec responded, "We just didn't know what we needed to spend money on back then. We spent a lot trying to understand the most effective way to reach our target audience. That is the key question and if you can answer that effectively, you can save yourself a ton of money."

In my experience, entrepreneurs tend to know how to develop their product in a cost-effective manner. It is often through the manner in which they *market* their product or service that entrepreneurs waste a great deal of resources (time, effort, and capital—human and financial) on trial and error. Take a look at some specific examples in exercise 1.7.

With every challenge, such as being undercapitalized, also comes the opportunity to scale a viable growth-oriented company upward. The fundamental question becomes: At what cost? What is the opportunity cost in the division, operations, and lifestyle nature of any organization that raises outside capital? I am often reminded of a mentor's wisdom: "Simply because you *can* doesn't mean that you *should*."

If you do, in fact, choose to journey down the fundraising path, it is critical that you understand that not all capital—or even every source of capital—is created equal. You will get countless opinions and personal

Exercise 1.7
Areas in Your Business to Be Frugal

Where could you be more frugal before, during, and after your fundraising campaign? Here are three areas to consider:

1. *Compensation.* Is your *entire* company on some type of performance-based compensation? If not, why not?

Most of the entrepreneurs we interviewed deeply believe in the "carrot" concept of enhanced compensation for those who deliver results.

2. *Suppliers.* Do you aggressively (but fairly) negotiate with your suppliers and find three go-to sources for your critical resources? If not, why not?

---

3. *Barter.* Can you take cash out of the equation by bartering your products and services to get what you need? Have you tried? If not, why not?

Here are a few other ways to save money:

- Tying resources to revenue performance
- Using independent contractors when and where appropriate
- Using summer interns and co-ops from area colleges and universities

At the next team meeting, sit down and come up with ten simple, frugal ideas you could implement. (Word of caution: Don't be penny-wise and pound-foolish.) Write your best ideas below:

---

perspectives. Keep in mind, though, that many are from the provider's lens. Your best bet is to leverage your portfolio of relationships to identify key individuals who have traveled the path before you. Reach out to as many entrepreneurs as possible and ask a simple question: If you knew *then* what you know *now*, what are the three things you would have done differently?

Another strong recommendation is to surround yourself with a board of advisors who have successfully raised your desired size and source of capital and can help guide you through the process. Look for retired CEOs and CFOs, corporate attorneys, and accountants with direct and relevant operating experience—those who "didn't paint their gray hairs on." They can help you avoid countless pitfalls along the journey.

One piece of advice you're certain to get is to "aim to raise *smart capital*." I first heard and understood the value of this term in the mid-1990s, and the lack of smart capital has become very clear in subsequent investment deals I've reviewed or board meetings I've participated in.

In the next chapter, we'll take a closer look at smart capital and how to stay away from less value-added versions.

SUMMARY

- ☑ Many types of businesses must raise capital to grow and scale profitably.
- ☑ Raising capital is as much about money as it is about finding and developing a strong relationship with a financial partner.
- ☑ Before you embark on the journey to raise capital, make certain you are clear about the intended use of that capital and your desired outcome from the investment.
- ☑ Every industry has a specific set of nuances, so be clear about the challenges or opportunities you're addressing, your target buyers, and that which makes your solution clearly unique.
- ☑ Economic conditions can present dynamics beyond your control; develop a set of proactive options to adapt to necessary changes.
- ☑ The timing, amount, and sources of capital you raise are critical.
- ☑ Quickly assess the gap between the people you have in critical roles and the ones you need for the evolution of the business.
- ☑ Raising capital can be complex, expensive, and time consuming.

2

Smart Capital

Not every type and source of capital is "smart." I have often witnessed undereducated and inexperienced investors become disruptive, if not destructive, to many CEOs in their efforts to grow their organizations. In addition, the "wrong" kind of capital can be equally destructive. You need to choose the *right* investors and the *right* kind of capital at the *right* time, and therefore it is critical to develop a litmus test or filtering mechanism for the "smart" capital you should raise.

CAPITAL CAN BE DUMB OR SMART

There are two different types of capital: smart or dumb. Let's take a closer look at how to define each.

Smart Capital

The key to your success will be to raise smart capital from experienced investors who are able to support your efforts to expand the business. When you can recruit the necessary executive talent to help guide the company in the right direction, you become more efficient and effective in your utilization of appropriate resources. Only a patient approach to building the business will create a clear path to success for all involved shareholders.

In my interviews with both entrepreneurs and investors, many voiced a similar definition for smart capital despite coming from the two different camps. Many entrepreneurs, for example, defined "smart" capital as funding that came with a unique and highly differentiated value addition provided by the *source* of that capital. In other words, astute investors made the capital smart by offering even more worthwhile benefits along with the money.

Often, questions of particular interest to entrepreneurs are:

- What do investors have to offer beyond the obvious business acumen?
- What is their relevant past experience in building and scaling a business?

- What are some of their best practices, including techniques to both survive the initial hard going and then thrive?
- Do they have access to a broad base of individuals at multiple levels who can be helpful?
- Can they introduce us to prospective customers, strategic partners, or other influential members of the business and investor community?

Many entrepreneurs also seek credibility by association. It seldom hurts to have retired military brass as investors and on your board when you are pursuing military contracts, for instance. Likewise, credible investors seldom hurt your chances for greater or easier access to potential high-profile board members.

Investors define smart capital slightly differently. Beyond what they can do for the entrepreneurs, investors look to provide "rocket boosters" to get a fledgling idea or business elevated above the market "noise." They do this primarily to protect their own investments. The investors I interviewed defined smart capital as money *plus*:

- individual mentoring opportunities to raise the CEO's business acumen and self-confidence to think and act bigger
- independent perspective and unique insights on the quality and appropriate fit of the entire leadership team and their ability to meet goals
- invitations to private events such as those held at the homes of highly respected industry luminaries, as well as valuable conferences such as the TED (Technology, Entertainment, Design) conference or the World Economic Forum's annual meeting in Davos, Switzerland
- advice on accelerating product development, thus conserving a great deal of cash and speeding up the time to market in the process
- lucrative alliance opportunities that can lead to investments by other strategic investors

So, whereas entrepreneurs might think of smart capital as "What else is in it for me?" investors perceive it as an opportunity to boost their most promising ventures and help them realize their full potential.

Exercise 2.1
Defining Your "Smart Capital"

How do you define "smart capital" in your particular situation? Think about this and capture a few characteristics that really define what that term means to your specific business. How would you know smart capital if you saw it?

_____
_____
_____
_____
_____

Dumb Capital

If we agree that the adjective *smart* describes a quantifiable added value beyond the capital itself, what are some examples of "less than smart" or outright "dumb" capital? Based on our interviews, here are some examples of dumb capital:

- *Capital that requires you to give up control of the company too early in the process.* In essence, you have bought yourself a job and face a high risk of someone else pulling the rug out from under you, often through no fault of your own. Without control, the dynamics of the company change, and you are less likely to reap the rewards and benefits that you have earned from fueling that growth. Unfortunately, entirely too many entrepreneurs give away too much of the company way too early in the fundraising cycle. One CEO we spoke with was fired shortly after raising capital and giving up control in the process. Not surprisingly, he used the severance package he had negotiated from the last company to fund a new company that did not want to raise equity from outside sources.
- *Capital that comes with intrusive investors and board members.* Investors and board members who are disruptive to the day-to-day operations and ask baseless questions tend to waste more valuable resources than they bring. I distinctly recall sitting in a board meeting in Manhattan where, well into the company's fourth year of operations, an angel investor pontificated for a few hours on a topic that the company had addressed two years earlier. With the next round of capital, he was bought out.
- *Capital providers who are not aligned with the cash flow dynamics of your business.* The cash flow dynamics of every industry are very different from the others. Savvy investors should be interested in whether the company will have sufficient cash flow to meet its needs. They are often very sophisticated in analyzing a company's need for cash, and most investors will carefully study a company's monthly cash flow projections before making an investment decision.

Here is how I define dumb money: poor timing between when you raise money and when you need to spend it for the greatest benefit to the business. Lack of money at the right time when the business needs it the most creates a disruption to the operations, which often postpones growing the business profitably.

Another example of going after dumb money is raising it from those who get personal or emotional about their investment. Instead, you want to raise capital from investors who are dispassionate about their money. Many times, angel investors, though they may be very wealthy, go through a personal crisis—such as a divorce—and all of a sudden need their money back. Institutional investors, on the other hand, are more likely to have the same end goal as you: appreciation of capital. You don't want contradicting agendas that create unnecessary stress and aggravation.

Capital should fuel your company for running the marathon—it should be nutritious food for the business. If some food gives you food poisoning, not only are you not training for the marathon, but you are out of the running altogether. Dumb capital has the same effect in this way: instead of supporting, enhancing, and enabling your development and growth, it creates more unnecessary friction, distraction, and bickering. Feel free to put this in the "life's too short" category.

Oil and water don't mix. There is an old saying, "Be careful whom you marry because you are also getting their family." This is also very true in raising capital. Be careful from whom you take money because, along with the money, you also get their individual pet peeves, prejudices, and critical assumptions—none of which may be relevant or applicable to you. But they certainly are part of the baggage that comes with capital.

There are countless other versions of dumb capital that could bite you during the due diligence phase or after you accept the capital (see chapter 10 for the top mistakes to avoid). So how do you avoid getting yourself into these situations?

KEEPING YOURSELF OUT OF THE DUMB MONEY POOL

Larry Bock of Lux Capital suggests that the ideal scenario is to bring in three to four high-quality first-tier (top-grade) investors from the very beginning. Even with his first company, with no track record as a proven entrepreneur, Larry approached first-tier investors because he knew that's what it would take to succeed. First-tier investors are often intelligent, engaging, and highly experienced. In Larry's case, five tier-one venture funds each put in $300,000, which is too small an amount for any of them to really get excited about. But because Larry and his team knew that the business was going to take a lot of money and a great deal of diverse expertise from the start, he built in the capability for subsequent rounds so that when he later had to raise $20 million, he was able to raise it from those who already knew, liked, and trusted him.

The fundamental challenge for most entrepreneurs when dealing with tier-one investors is that these investors have a heightened sensitivity for half-truths. We all start out with a certain level of perceived credibility, but unfortunately many entrepreneurs shoot themselves in the foot and dilute, if not destroy, that credibility before they even walk in the door.

Trustworthy investors:

- are congruent in what they say and what they do,
- hold positive reputations,
- have a past history of quality deal-flow and investment success stories, and
- possess a catalog of "lessons learned" from less-than-stellar investment performers.

This is, in part, what gives them the ability to discern poor risks with apparent ease. In our experience, tier-one investors tend to associate with and are referred by other tier-one investors and intermediaries (see chapter 9 for more on consultants, investment bankers, and intermediaries).

It is critical in your fundraising campaign to map out a strategic relationship plan. In this plan resides a traditional three-step process of identifying the current state and future state and the gap between them, coupled with a fresh perspective on the quantifiable and strategic value of business relationships.

Let's take a closer look at each.

Step One: Define Your Current State

Begin with an independent and highly introspective view of where your business is today. Gather accurate and updated financials, sufficient market research, and details on your unique position in the marketplace. Review your current strategic and tactical operating strengths and weaknesses. Be completely honest with yourself: Where do you stand?

It is critical to not jump ahead and think of solutions or get defensive, but rather to focus on the present. What hard and soft assets do you possess that could be perceived as being of great value to prospective investors? What infrastructure do you currently possess that will allow you to build a scalable model? What are the critical assumptions you are making about key individuals or pieces of information that could make or break your company?

Step Two: Define Your Future State

An old friend once told me, "Think big, start small, scale fast."

The future state is the "think big" part. Can you succinctly articulate and credibly convince others of the realistic potential of your business? Keep in mind that not every business can reach $100 million or $500 million in revenue and compete in $50 billion markets. Your aim here is for them to believe you today and believe in you tomorrow.

An accurate forecast—given the often multiple rounds of investments and an infusion of capital (both financial and human)—should allow you to extrapolate a realistic company position in the market. The believability of that position—the credibility and accuracy of that position—will depend on the critical assumptions and performance milestones you map out along the continuum. Traditional hockey-stick growth models (steep and quickly achieved trajectories) are rare and are therefore less believable to savvy investors.

Step Three: Define the Gap

The gap between where you are currently and where you can realistically be in the future becomes your *scalability plan*. How will you reach that desirable future? What kind of people do you need? What kind of machinery or infrastructure? What new skills and capabilities? It is often difficult to define the slope. Amongst everything else that must happen, six or eight critical "betting the business" milestones will help make the rise more bite-size and the run more digestible in the process.

In any scalability plan, attention to the following points is critical to your success.

- *"One-offs" will kill you.* If it's not repeatable and predictable in a process environment, don't do it. Avoid doing anything just once—whether for employees, suppliers, customers, or investors.
- *Clearly delineate roles and responsibilities, leveraging the fundamental strengths of different players on the team.* To quote Jim Collins of *Good to Great: Why Some Companies Make the Leap—and Others Don't* (2001) fame, "Get the right people on the bus and in the right seats." In my experience, a number of early-stage companies struggle in their scalability plan when that scalability is on the shoulders of B- and C-caliber employees incapable of carrying the responsibility or authority to execute.
- *Avoid the "trunk and branch" mentality.* Most companies start with a focused effort, a highly targeted market, and a succinct value proposition. Think of these as the trunk of the tree. As products or services expand, branches begin to grow. But if they grow too far away from the trunk—the core strength—difficult economic conditions will break off such branches, like a tree in a storm, causing the company to struggle.
- *Don't forget your roots.* While I'm on the trunk-and-branch analogy, here's some wisdom my father passed along to me: "Don't forget where you come from." Often, your early customers and alliance partners can become the key to your success. Make sure they are not left behind and that you proactively engage the relevant ones as your business evolves.
- *Performance trumps all.* Beyond lofty projections, your ability to consistently perform, execute, and deliver both quantitative and qualitative performance will infuse much-needed credibility to both the broader plan and your ability to get there.

Exercise 2.2
Scalability Challenges

What are the top three challenges keeping you from scaling your business? By *scale*, I mean the organization's ability to grow profitably without you having to do everything.

Here is a test for you to ponder: Can you afford to go away—*really* get away—from the business for a week? A month? Four to six months? Will it still be there when you get back? In better or worse shape? How do you know?

GREENER PASTURES

If you should find yourself having raised what we are calling less-than-smart capital, the sooner you get out of it, the better. In many instances, the detriments of dumb capital will tend to get worse before they get better, often leading to emotionally charged disagreements rather than a logical, productive dialogue of what is really best for the business.

Leveraging relationships with existing investors to buy out the less-than-desirable ones is politically, financially, and legally challenging. The process is not for the faint of heart. Many of the entrepreneurs I interviewed attested to being at the brink of disaster in dealing with this scenario.

In subsequent *rounds of financing*, the process of cleaning up your *CAP table* should be objective, but often is not. *Dilution* created by a flat valuation—or worse yet, a *down round*—can cause significant emotional heartache for early investors. (See the sidebar for definitions of the words in italics. A more detailed description of the concepts will be found in chapter 8.)

Critical Definitions

Rounds of financing	Multiple investment events during a company's growth cycle. Common terms include *friends & family*; *angel*; A, B, C, D, etc. (for the successive rounds of true institutional investors); and *mezzanine*.
CAP table	A table breaking down the percentage or equity owned by a variety of investors, segmented by *available*, *issued*, *preferred*, and *common* shares.
Dilution	A decrease in percentage or actual value in the company's stock represented by the additional/subsequent shares purchased by an investor.
Down round	Reduced valuation in the company after subsequent investment events.
Limited partner (LP)	A private investment group such as a pension fund, insurance company, or corporate investor, that invests in private equity and venture capital funds.

Years ago, early investors—the first money in—set the rules of any investment deal. But with the burst of the Internet bubble, when a great number of companies lost their often hyperinflated valuations, subsequent investors came into the deal and often reset a company's valuation at a fraction of that of the previous rounds. As a result, all past investors lost a significant equity position in the deal (imagine a $100 investment you make in a company for 10 percent equity now being worth $1 or less). But in an effort to stay afloat and continue operations, many businesses were forced to take subsequent financing at considerably reduced valuations. Hence the new paradigm: "Last money in sets the rules."

Near the end of the 2000 bubble, Alec Peters raised $5 million in angel investments for his company, Auctionworks. "I loved working with angels and would write them a monthly update to keep them informed on our progress," Alec recalls. "If you wind up with the wrong VC, and remember, all they care about is THEIR money and not necessarily you, it will tear down your company and every investor before them will suffer. A bad VC will generally drive out the founders and ruin the corporate culture."

At his new company, Alec has raised $1.2 million from a venture capitalist (VC) with whom he has a long-term relationship. Because Alec had an established relationship with the firm before he accepted its money, this has been a successful and highly supportive experience thus far.

Another entrepreneur shared her story of a twenty-four-month cycle in which she jumped through countless hoops—all with extensive consulting and legal expenses—to pursue an investor. Though this investor had passed the "smell test" (he had all the right appearances, contacts, and perceptions of legitimacy), in reality he was in no position to invest even a fraction of the previously discussed and agreed-upon capital. In addition to losing the investment opportunity, she lost more than two years of expanding her business in the community.

As with most investment scenarios, there is often more than one perspective. Although venture capital is often labeled smart money, several entrepreneurs with less-than-ideal outcomes in their venture-backed businesses complained of seeing the VCs only for periodic board meetings. Their perception was that a great majority of VCs are more interested and committed to an internal rate of return than to adding value. Conversely, the angel money they raised—some as much as $10 million—was generally considered being less intrusive, more supportive, and more proactive in the evolution of the business.

Many believe that what institutional venture funds attempt to portray is "active money," though whether as a positive or negative is an open question. The money behind the venture firms—that of their limited partners—can also create a perceived conflict of interest between the need for attractive returns on invested capital and the need of the entrepreneur for steady, prudent growth. The VC's fundamental and fiduciary responsibility to an entrepreneur as a member of the board could fall victim to its fiscal obligation to its limited partners. Some call this "seagull management": the practice of "flying in, crapping on you, and flying back out again" (as stated by one entrepreneur interviewed).

One of the best resources for entrepreneurs is www.thefunded.com, an independent source of information where entrepreneurs contribute great insights regarding their investor experiences at varying stages of their company's growth.

Exercise 2.3
How Much Money Will You Require?

How much funding will your business require? At what incremental or exponential stages of your growth?

_____

_____

How will you prioritize this infusion of capital, and how will you measure its effective and efficient use?

_____

_____

_____

In the next chapter, we'll focus on strategic financial planning, a process familiar to many, but practiced by few!

SUMMARY

- ☑ Not every type and source of capital is "smart."
- ☑ Smart capital is characterized by a unique and highly differentiated added value provided by the source and use of that capital.
- ☑ Dumb capital is characterized by entrepreneurs giving up too much control too early in the process, inviting uneducated or intrusive investors in the business, and misaligning investment objectives with that of the business.
- ☑ To avoid the dumb money pool, develop a strategic relationship plan to attract tier-one investors.
- ☑ A scalability plan is developed through a three-step process: identify the current state, identify the desired future state, and identify the gap between where your business is today and where you're trying to take it.
- ☑ Find ways to test your strategy, invest in key people to help execute your strategy, build repeatable processes, and stay focused on performance and results—particularly financial projections.
- ☑ If you raise less-than-smart money, leverage your relationship with stronger investors to replace the less-than-desirable ones.
- ☑ Leverage the insights and experiences of other entrepreneurs who have previously raised capital successfully to avoid similar mistakes.

3

Plan Now or Pay Later

Beyond identifying the type and source of the most appropriate capital, a critical—yet often misunderstood and poorly applied—process is the financial stewardship of that capital for the greatest return on that limited asset.

STRATEGIC FINANCIAL PLANNING

Strategic financial planning not only identifies and aligns the strategic business goals of today with the required capital but also anticipates the capital infusion required to meet the business execution challenges of tomorrow.

There is a familiar refrain among investors when it comes to looking at your business and deciding whether or not to invest: What are the opportunities for growth? Be it a bank or private equity firm, investors want to see where you are going as much as where you have been. A solid set of projections is crucial for any business seeking capital.

Unfortunately, very few entrepreneurs engage in the process of anticipating their financial requirements using what-if scenarios—both positive and negative. It is critical to differentiate traditional financial forecasting—most of which is often pulled out of thin air—with strategic financial planning, which means aligning business requirements and milestones strategically with the appropriate and required capital infusion. Of particular importance is anticipating possible future events based on extensive industry experience, subject matter or domain knowledge, and the ability to predict how your business will react to varying trends and take the appropriate actions.

Intelligent anticipation of the business's trajectory and the cause and effect of each enabler or stumbling block can require different uses of capital. The key is to understand:

- at what cost,
- for what tradeoff, and
- to what end.

What will be the cost of capital today versus when you anticipate that need? What will be the fundamental tradeoffs of investing capital in one direction of the business versus another? What is the desired end result? Intelligent anticipation can dramatically decrease potential risk. But more importantly, it can decrease the surprise of financial events, which are detrimental to most growing businesses.

If planning a path and aligning business milestones with the required capital infusion is such an obvious proposition, why do so few entrepreneurs extend their vision, mission, and strategy into a strategic financial plan and tie accountability and the initiatives of key members of the team back to that strategy?

The truth is that many are so busy running the day-to-day operations of the business that they do not invest the time to plan their financial futures strategically. They then often end up reaching a crisis point in their burn rate (a negative cash-flow situation in which the company is spending more money than it generates).

Exercise 3.1
Critical Milestones Ahead

What are the three to five critical milestones for your business over the next twenty-four to thirty-six months? Be specific (e.g., "Version 1.0 of this software application by October 1," "Second retail location in Midtown by November 10," etc.).

1. _____
2. _____
3. _____
4. _____
5. _____

WHAT IS STRATEGIC FINANCIAL PLANNING?

Strategic financial planning is often misunderstood. Let me tell you what strategic financial planning is *not*, as well as explaining what it *is*, using its key characteristics.

Length

A strategic financial plan is not a 40- to 100-page dissertation that few will ever read. A strategic financial plan is often no more than five pages long. (Many investors told us it should be only one page! Describing the "so what" of your product, solution, offering, or company in one page is the best way to get an investor's attention.) Summarize in the plan your business ideas and offerings in the context of the market's fundamental challenges; why buyers would choose your solutions; and how will they become aware of the products or services, try them, tell their friends and colleagues, and come back for more.

Tradition

A strategic financial plan is not five-year traditional pro forma modeling. Early on, you don't know enough to project that far out. Because much of the traditional financial projections is based on critical assumptions, if you haven't thought through many of those assumptions, and if they are not credible, you can do more to damage rather than strengthen your reputation if you try to project extensive pro forma models too far into the future.

Content

A strategic financial plan is not a lot of numbers without context. For the nonfinancial participants or those simply allergic to spreadsheets, most traditional financial planning makes little or no sense if the content is based more on formulas than on demonstrable progress.

If, Then

Traditional plans outline things in the form "If this happens, then this is what we would do." Strategic financial planning is focused, instead, on "Why not this?" For example, a typical plan might say, "If we hire X sales reps, we will then win Y customers and generate this much revenue." Instead, a strategic financial plan should help in asking questions such as: "How else can we disrupt the current value chain in taking our products and services to market?" "What about a 'user' sales force?" "Why not blur the line between producers and consumers and leverage social networks to drive awareness?"

Audience

Traditional financial planning is done by number crunchers for number crunchers. A strategic financial plan is as much a marketing plan that ties the vision with personal initiatives as it is a bunch of numbers. The audience is not just prospective investors but also potential key members of the management team you need to recruit, as well as influential members of the business, media, and political community at large.

ALTERNATIVE TO TRADITIONAL FIVE-YEAR FINANCIAL MODELS

As mentioned above, in the early stages, you simply don't have enough meaningful information to create five-year financial models. As such, your strategic financial plan should succinctly identify the following five key areas:

1. *Eight to ten critical milestones in the company's evolution.* To get venture capital funding, you must invest in powerful ideas. Do you really

believe no one else thought of music on memory sticks before the invention of the iPod? Similarly, what do you think the recently announced Kleiner Perkins iFund, which has earmarked $100 million to invest in applications to run on the iPhone, is looking for? Investors of all sizes, calibers, industries, and geographic foci believe in an idea and plan to capitalize on it through market-defining products and best-in-class, industry-leading companies.

In the previous chapter, we discussed your perception of your business's future state. What are the eight or ten critical steps that will get you to that future state? It is important here that your thinking and articulation of those critical milestones are not based on current physical limitations. Don't limit yourself by heights that have been reached in the past. Instead, broaden the potential and possibility in what could be done.

2. *Financial stewardship to reach the next milestone.* Here is where legitimate, credible financial metrics and performance will be crucial. Think of each milestone as a building block. What financial resources will you need to get there? What are the prioritized investments that will lead the business to the milestone with the highest level of predictability and mitigated risk? Balance a frugal approach to investing with the appropriate timeline and horizon to allow for sufficient trial-and-error market development, acceptance, and scale.

Figure 3.1
Strategic Financial Planning—Expected Input

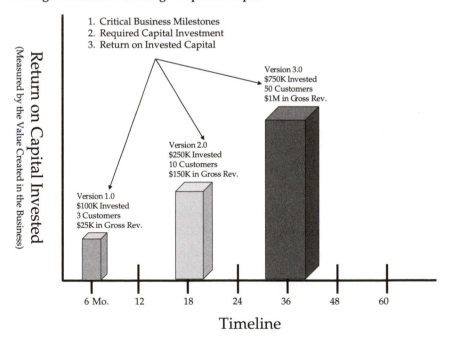

3. *Required capital and use of those resources at that point in time.* Market dynamics change at each critical milestone. A savvy entrepreneur, along with external and internal advisors, should plan on the sources and amounts of capital that will be required at each of those milestones. That entrepreneur will prioritize the use of that capital to create a trajectory to the next milestone. Again, develop a long enough lead time not only to get the products and services off the ground but also to create awareness and to try and repeat opportunities for your target market.

4. *Anticipated capital infusion for low, medium, and high estimates.* Different market dynamics will shift both the timing of achieving your milestone as well as its perceived impact. In my experience, there are three points to anticipate—low, medium, and high scenarios—on both the timeline horizon and the impact barometer, and each will require a different level of capital infusion. Each may also produce a different level of capital performance. For example, your new product could be released in March, June, or October of next year. It could sell 100 units, 10,000 units, or 10 million units. Producing, marketing, selling, and delivering on those metrics at different times will require different levels of capital.

Figure 3.2
Strategic Financial Planning—Desired Output

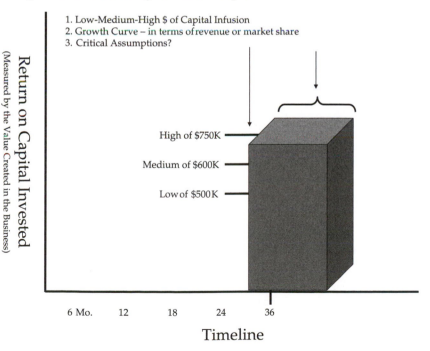

5. *Standard deviations, both plus and minus, on each milestone.* In the previous example, March-June-October forms a bell curve. You must also understand not only what you should be doing, but what the best use of capital at different points in that bell curve is and what you will do if that curve shifts. Will you need more people in distribution? More people in customer service? Will you have the spare parts you need? If we didn't learn anything else from Hurricane Katrina and its aftermath in New Orleans, we learned that you better have not only plan A but also plans B, C, and D. Many entrepreneurs have limited sources—they spec out a product or service based on what they get from suppliers. Flexibility in thinking about the process adds different scenarios, options, and avenues.

Exercise 3.2
Critical Milestones, Anticipated Capital Needs, and Expected Results

For each of the three to five critical milestones you captured in exercise 3.1, write the low, medium, and high (L-M-H) levels of capital infusion necessary in the second column and the expected result from that investment in the third column.

Critical Business Milestones	Required Capital (L-M-H)	Expected Result ($ revenue increase or cost savings)
1.		
2.		
3.		
4.		
5.		

If you were an independent investor, would you give yourself the capital in column 2 above to produce the results in column 3? Why or why not? Be specific, independent, and candid.

_____
_____
_____
_____

WHY DON'T MORE PEOPLE DO IT?

Here are seven of the top reasons most entrepreneurs fail to plan strategically.

1. *Lack of financial or strategic astuteness.* Many entrepreneurs are not financially astute. They don't think about textbook business plans. They know how to hustle, how to put together a business, and how to manage people and are always looking at how they can make a buck—but putting the numbers on paper isn't necessarily their core competency.
2. *Lack of experience.* Like anything else that is not routine, very few people have the experience to approach the problem for the first time from a position of great wisdom. However, because they have experience, serial entrepreneurs are often in a better position to provide quality analysis. They possess a more intuitive sense of what's around the corner, whereas seeing around the corner can be tricky for someone who has never raised capital before.

   In the technology sector, many company founders are engineers focused on moving their products forward and are not tuned in to strategic financial planning. Often, entrepreneurs put their friends and families—many of whom can add little or no value—on their boards of advisors or directors and in important functional areas such as sales, marketing, and strategic business development, all of which need experts to serve in advisory roles.

   Entrepreneurs who are raising capital for the second or third time tend to plan ahead strategically. They think about long-term viability and competitive forks in the road where they might need to add or consolidate their product offerings. But first-time entrepreneurs are more focused on what is happening in the company in the present, which is often all-encompassing to them.
3. *Reinventing the wheel.* Many entrepreneurs are hell-bent on "reinventing the wheel" from scratch. They attempt to reinvent processes that many have already figured out before them.
4. *Flawed assumptions.* Sometimes entrepreneurs *think* they are doing strategic financial planning, but their plans are totally unrealistic. Businesses that need money are usually in that position for a reason. As the cliché goes, "If you do what you've always done, you will get what you've always got."
5. *Traumas in daily life.* Most entrepreneurs approach the idea of strategic planning in a logical and optimistic way without recognizing the broad range of traumas that may confront their business in real life. Without digging deep and truly evaluating risk, trend analysis is not enough and will miss the point.
6. *Personal lens.* Paradigms constructed from one's personal experiences are often myopic. Individuals tend to view life through their own personal lens, but not all investors have the same view of the market. As such, investors can view the same set of issues very differently. Hence, an entrepreneur can get a very different set of results from the same set of inputs, depending on who is in the driver's seat.

7. *No encouragement from the investment community.* Investment cycles tend to have certain characteristics. For example, a *flip cycle* is one during which many investors get in and then sell the business within the next two years. As such, doing an in-depth level of strategic financial planning is not perceived to be of value. Another cycle is one of "We're not sure what the growth is going to look like, so let's just get to the next level."

Today, very few investors stick with the same thing for ten or fifteen years. Many see strategic entrepreneurs as an intelligent group taking a path of least resistance. Instead of picking up a phone and talking to the customer or taking out a second mortgage on their house to finance the company, it is perceived to be much easier for many entrepreneurs to take their time to build a great business plan. Ultimately, however, few investors care. They are looking for the entrepreneur to build a company and have something to sell.

Typically, those who don't think strategically about the future don't have an investor encouraging them to think that way, nor do they have the experience that tells them they need to do so. That is why investors value entrepreneurs with a track record—someone who has done it before and has perspective from doing it from beginning to end. Still, you can learn to overcome any of these hindrances and create or expand a business that is attractive to investors.

Exercise 3.3
Strategic Financial Planning

If you're not doing strategic financial planning, why not? Be candid and capture some thoughts about what's keeping you from thinking and executing in this manner.

_____
_____
_____
_____

If you *are* consistently aligning the strategic business milestones with the need for critical infusion of capital, what are three areas in which you could improve your intelligent anticipation of key trends ahead of the curve?

_____
_____
_____
_____
_____

WHO DOES IT WELL AND WHY?

One entrepreneur I know runs a payday lending company. I found it quite interesting that, for what could be perceived as a low-tech business, this entrepreneur is constantly building financial models for different scenarios in the company's ability to add product lines or even additional stores in order to determine the potential cash impact on the business. The kind of financing the business requires at each strategic business milestone will heavily depend on which scenarios it is able to execute.

Here are some best practices we have found among other companies that are successful in their strategic financial planning:

- *Automate the process.* Those who do it well automate the entire process. There are macros in Excel and other spreadsheet programs, and there is business planning simulation software out there as well. To the maximum extent possible, figure out how to automate the process.
- *Make it a living document.* Unfortunately, many financial plans go on a shelf and that's where they stay until eleven months, three weeks, and four and a half days later. If it's a living playbook and the players change, you should be able to give the plan to the new players and they should be able to quickly grasp it without negatively affecting the business.
- *Socialize your plan.* One entrepreneur had a one-year strategic financial plan on a notepad stuck to the door of his office. Everyone who walked by saw what the company was doing, where they were headed, and what had to happen for them to get there. The company rallied around the plan with a sense of communal accomplishment.
- *Make it a highly visual representation.* One entrepreneur built his plan as a permanent fixture on the company's intranet with a dashboard-like progress report (similar to the dashboard of instruments in your car), measuring a range of critical milestones, making it a highly visual representation. The financial metrics were just one of the key performance indicators against which to measure the strategic business goals and milestones for which the team was aiming.
- *Match contributors with recipients.* Different people contribute to writing a strategic financial plan, and they each come to it with unique perspectives. Match that perspective with investors looking for that same perspective and communication style. For example, an analytical person who writes the financial model would be best aligned with an analytical investor interested in dissecting the model. On the other hand, a highly expressive chief marketing officer needs to engage an equally expressive creative counterpart with capital to invest.
- *Hire the right CFO.* It is important to hire a strategic chief financial officer who can balance critical milestones with their financial implications. One of the most desirable aspects in a prospective CFO should be that they can serve as a business enabler and not a business inhibitor.

Remember: Don't get bogged down with a ton of financial modeling. It's critical to stay focused on selling the ideas and mapping those ideas with intelligent anticipation of where you are going and what it will take to get you there. The clear, concise, and consistent communication of that living plan with your investors is vital.

SUMMARY

☑ Strategic financial planning identifies and aligns the strategic business goals of today with the required capital.

☑ Strategic financial planning appropriately anticipates the capital infusion required to exceed the business execution challenges of tomorrow.

☑ The three critical questions to ask when developing a strategic financial plan are about the cost, the tradeoffs, and the ends to be achieved.

☑ Strategic financial planning is not valued by its length. Shorter is better.

☑ Strategic financial planning is not valued by traditional financial pro forma models created by number crunchers for financial engineers.

☑ Strategic financial planning should focus on the next three to five critical milestones ahead in the business, strategic and independent questions about what the business is aiming to accomplish, and the financial resources it will need to get there.

☑ A "Low-Medium-High" approach to critical assumptions in both business goals and capital requirements makes the plan more credible and thus believable to prospective investors.

☑ Many entrepreneurs don't engage in strategic financial planning for several reasons: lack of knowledge or skills, a narrow personal lens of market dynamics, flawed assumptions, or a lack of encouragement from the investment community.

☑ Entrepreneurs who build strong, strategic financial plans automate the process, create living documents, leverage internal and external resources, make it highly visual, and hire strategic CFOs.

☑ Clear, consistent communication to the investors of updates to a living strategic financial plan becomes a strong asset in building your credibility and track record.

4

Bootstrapping and Early-Stage Creative Capital

Some of the least expensive and most accessible early sources of capital (or what is often referred to as "seed capital") can come from your own bootstrapping efforts. This includes short-term loans from individuals who already know and trust you, such as family and friends, and from highly influential local relationships in your professional circles. Some CPAs, attorneys, doctors, real estate agents, and friends can often provide the financial seed money to launch and expand any company.

SEED CAPITAL AND BOOTSTRAPPING TO GET YOU THERE

Many entrepreneurs have business ideas that may take years to develop into a salable product and will require millions of dollars in invested capital to get there. Obviously, for these entrepreneurs, seed capital from external sources won't work. But they may have access to more capital than they think. If their idea is that strong, the investment of their own money will be prudent and will pay off. Early on is also when the business is at its lowest value, so bootstrapping allows entrepreneurs to avoid giving away too much too early in the lifecycle.

Exercise 4.1
Your Access to Liquid Cash

How much cash could you access if you added up the credit limits of all your credit cards? How about your home equity line of credit, the cash value of your insurance policies, and the money in your 401(k)?

_____

_____

As there is always a cost of capital, what would be the aggregate annual percentage rate of using this capital? _____

_____

Many entrepreneurs opt to take only a modest sum of early investments and instead rely primarily on sales and real customer revenues. This was a novel concept in the late 1990s during the venture capital surge, but one that "old school" experience assured would offer the most opportunity and flexibility. It was the option that ultimately guaranteed the founders the healthiest stake in the company. Before venture capital funding came along, if real customers didn't buy your idea, there was no way to generate cash and keep operating. Without a demonstrated sales history, no bank would even talk to you.

The same principle applies today. Unfortunately, we see way too many companies lose their focus. They don't develop a strategy to optimize their sales and revenue growth efforts.

The effort is worth it, though. With sales and profitability, you exponentially increase your chances for acquiring seed capital. The journey may take a bit longer when a business relies on customer revenues to pay its bills. But these bootstrapped ventures realize their success when they hit critical mass in revenue—for many it's $5 million or more in revenue. They soon realize they need to raise growth capital if they are to efficiently scale their sales and marketing organization—a critical step for continued growth.

Bridge loans as short-term borrowing vehicles can fund a company's operations for a specific period of time, often as an interim step before longer-term financing can be secured. The good—and bad—news about borrowing money is that there are many different loan options and, while the money is out there, it is often confusing to decide which path is right for you.

Many loans fund only very specific capital expenditures. Here's a quick breakdown of some sources of capital to consider:

- *Business plan competitions.* University- or industry association-sponsored contests are popping up all over the country. Business-founding participants are required to be current students, recent graduates, or teams that include at least one university student.
- *Grants.* Many government agencies provide low-interest loans or outright grants. These agencies can also offer frameworks and ideas. They are actively seeking organizations to which they can award grants. More details on government agencies will be covered in chapter 5.
- *Innovation contests.* The Intellectual Property Owners Association, for example, awards $5,000 to one inventor each year. The Lemelson-MIT Awards offer $500,000 to an individual, $30,000 to a student, and $30,000 to a student team with a patent. The Chrysler Design Award gives six $10,000 grants to winners in the categories of urban design, graphic design, landscaping, architecture, new media, and fashion.
- *Supplier financing.* For example, a swimsuit business I know received $1 million in financial backing from the manufacturer.
- *Low-interest SBA loans.* The Small Business Administration (SBA) backs various types of small-business loans made through local banks and agencies. (Don't even bother looking into this if you don't have a financial track record, however.) These loans can be used to buy equipment,

inventory, furniture, supplies, and more. According to the SBA's website (www.sba.gov/financing), here's what you'll need:

1. Business profile: A document describing the type of business you own, your annual sales, number of employees, length of time you've been in business, and ownership details.
2. Loan request: A description of how the loan funds will be used. This should include the purpose, amount, and type of loan you're looking for.
3. Collateral: A description of the items you're offering to secure the loan, including equity in the business, borrowed funds, and available cash.
4. Business financial statements: Complete financial statements for the past three years and current interim financial statements. The most important documents in your financial statements are your year-end balance sheets and income statements revealing your business profits or losses for the last three fiscal years. You will also need cash-flow projections indicating how much cash you expect to generate to repay the loan, as well as accounts receivable and payable aging reports, which break your receivables and payables into 30-, 60-, 90-, and past-90-day-old categories.
5. Personal financial statements: Statements of owners, partners, officers, and stockholders owning 20 percent or more of the business that list all personal assets, liabilities, and monthly payments, as well as copies of your personal tax returns for the past three years.

- *Line-of-credit loans.* These are short-term loans that allow you to access a specific amount of money, often transferred to your business checking account the same day. You pay a predetermined market rate on the money you borrow. I've used them as working capital to pay operating costs, but you generally can't use them to buy real estate or equipment.
- *Revolving lines of credit.* Think of these as corporate credit cards: a bank offers a certain limit of money that can be borrowed over and over again, assuming you pay off the debt on time.

Exercise 4.2
Credible Financial Statements

How accurate and credible are your financial statements? Next to delivering value for customers, close attention to your financial health and stewardship should be your number-two priority! Unfortunately, this isn't a lot of fun for most entrepreneurs—many rank it right up there with getting a root canal. So, get proactive and answer the following critical questions:

1. How often do you review your standard financial reports?

_____

_____

2. Is your accounting system able to scale with you?

_____

_____

(continued)

Exercise 4.2 *(continued)*

3. What are your plans B, C, and D if Bob the Bookkeeper isn't around anymore?

_____

_____

4. Can you access an advisor to help regularly review your financial state?

_____

_____

5. If independent investors were to review your financials, what would be their top three to five concerns? What are your candid, legitimate, and nondefensive responses to each?

a. _____

b. _____

c. _____

d. _____

e. _____

_____

Prepare and update your financial statements carefully, as they are often the primary basis for the lending decision. By the way, the SBA qualifying standards are more flexible than other types of loans, but lenders will generally prequalify you for an SBA loan program by asking for specific information.

The reason many entrepreneurs like debt financing is that it is the least expensive source of financing you can get. Consider the returns you can get from bank financing versus subordinated debt, equity, or even friends and family, who are going to want a return for their investment—generally above what a loan rate would be.

Subordinated debt is the next cheapest option. This is generally debt that is *subordinated* to the senior lender—usually a mechanism whereby the debt can be converted to equity under certain scenarios—but the return to the lender is not as high as with an equity provider. The benefit to this kind of capital is that, although it requires the use of equity, you are not giving up as much control as you would if you strictly raised equity funding.

Equity is generally the most expensive source of financing for a company—not to mention requiring you to give up more of the company than many entrepreneurs would prefer. As such, equity would be the third choice of these options.

The following is the basic process you should expect when working with a commercial banker:

1. *Meet.* A preliminary meeting takes place with the commercial bankers to allow them to gain an understanding of your requirements.
2. *Provide information.* Allow them to gather enough information to get an initial read on whether you and your business are attractive to them and whether your financial requirement is feasible under their internal guidelines.

3. *Assessment.* Generally they will get back to you within a few days if it looks like something they want to proceed with.
4. *Acceptance or declining.* If the application is accepted, the bankers will then produce a term sheet (see figure 4.1), spelling out details of the deal in simple terms. If not, they should still get back to you quickly with reasons why your deal is not acceptable, ideally offering some potential alternatives.
5. *Closing.* If the term sheet is acceptable to you, you move to closing. The duration depends on the complexity of the deal; typically, it takes between three and four weeks to close. A real estate deal may take longer due to appraisals, environmental issues, and so on.

Figure 4.1
Sample Term Sheet from a Corporate Banker

GENERIC CORPORATION

Outline of Terms and Conditions
Up to a $30,000,000 Senior Secured Credit Facility

Date

The following summary of terms and conditions should not be construed as a commitment to lend. This term sheet is for the purpose of outlining the proposed facilities. The definitive terms and conditions upon which Generic Bank might extend credit to the Borrower are subject to satisfactory completion of due diligence, final credit approval, satisfactory review and execution of documentation and such other terms and conditions as may be determined by Generic Bank and its counsel.

Lender: Generic Bank

Borrower(s): Generic Corporation and any relevant subsidiaries.

Facility I: Up to a $20,000,000 Revolving Credit Facility for working capital and capital expenditure needs subject to a Margin Requirement. Facility I may also be used to fund Approved Acquisitions as defined in the term sheet.
Three year credit facility.

Facility II: Up to $10 million in a non-revolving credit facility ("Cash Flow Loan") to finance other projects outside of Borrower's working capital needs including, but not limited to, capital expenditures and Approved Acquisitions. The availability of Facility II shall be governed by a cash flow leverage covenant (the "Cash Flow Leverage Covenant"). Facility II shall be structured with a 13 month rolling maturity. Any amounts funded under the facility shall be amortized for a term of up to 24 months beginning the first day of the next calendar quarter after funding. Facility II shall terminate at the same time as Facility I.

(continued)

Figure 4.1 *(continued)*

Security: First and only lien on all assets to include but not limited
                       to Accounts Receivable, Payment Intangibles, Inventory,
                       Equipment, Patents, General Intangibles, and Balances.
                       Lender reserves the right to file an assignment on selected
                       U.S. Government Contracts under the Assignment of
                       Claims Act of 1940.

Guarantor: The Facilities shall be cross-defaulted and cross-
                       collateralized.

Margin   Availability and eligibility criteria and appropriate advance
Requirement: caps will be based on due diligence results and a field
                       examination performed by the Lender. Gross Collateral
                       Availability shall generally be:
                       (1) Up to 90% of eligible accounts receivable from Prime
                           US Government contracts, plus
                       (2) Up to 85% of eligible accounts receivable from Prime
                           Contractors under US Government contracts, plus
                       (3) Up to 80% of eligible commercial accounts receivable
                           plus
                       (4) Up to 70% of eligible unbilled US Government accounts
                           (defined below) with a mutually agreeable cap
                       Ineligible accounts would include, but not be limited
                       to, accounts greater than 90 days past invoice, contras,
                       foreign accounts (certain foreign accounts may be pre-
                       approved for advance with appropriate advance rates and
                       caps to be determined), accounts subject to financial or
                       completion bonds, retainage, progress billings and cross-
                       aged accounts.

Interest Rate: A pricing matrix based on fixed charge coverage and tested
                       quarterly shall determine the Applicable Margin for each
                       Rate. Base Rate shall be Lender's Prime Rate.
                       Facility I:
                       Applicable Margin Matrix for Base Rate   00%
                       Applicable Margin Matrix for LIBOR   1.50% to 2.50%
                       Facility II:
                       50 basis points higher than the Matrix

Up-Front Fee: $100,000

Other Fees: Unused Fee of 0.25% on Facilities I & II.
                       Standby Letter of Credit Fees equal to the LIBOR-based
                       Applicable Margin.

Figure 4.1 *(continued)*

Financial Covenants:	To be measured quarterly, on a consolidated, rolling twelve-month basis. Covenants would include, but not be limited to, the following: • Minimum Fixed Charge Coverage Ratio • Maximum Capital Expenditures • Cash Flow Leverage Covenant (used only if Facility II is funded): • Maximum Funded Debt to TTM EBITDA
Other Covenants:	Usual and customary for transactions of this nature, and subject to limitations and exceptions otherwise provided for in this Term Sheet to be mutually agreed upon, including, but not limited to, limitations on additional indebtedness, liens, investments, mergers and consolidations, acquisitions, asset sales, transactions with affiliates, negative pledges, restricted payments, distributions, and dividends.
Financial Reporting:	All satisfactory to Lender: *Financial Reporting:* Annual Audited Financial Statements Monthly Financial Statements Quarterly Backlog Reports Quarterly Financial Covenant Compliance Certificate Financial projections presenting monthly and annual forecasts *Collateral Reporting for Facility I:* Monthly Borrowing Base Certificate setting the Margin Monthly Aging of Accounts Receivable and Accounts Payable
Approved Acquisitions:	The credit facilities may be used to fund the purchase of targeted acquisitions under the following general terms and conditions. Specific terms and conditions in greater detail would be outlined in any future loan documentation: • Target is in substantially the same business and industry. • The scope, execution, and results of Borrower's due diligence on Target are satisfactory to Lender. • Target has historical positive EBITDA at levels satisfactory to Lender. • Borrower demonstrates to Lender pro-forma compliance with financial covenants or agrees to new covenants satisfactory to Lender. • Funding from Facility I shall not impair working capital adequacy for the combined entity on a pro-forma basis.

(continued)

Figure 4.1 *(continued)*

- Total sources and types of funding used in the acquisition are satisfactory to Lender.
- All documentation shall be satisfactory to Lender including filing of satisfactory liens on new collateral.

Conditions Precedent and Other Matters:

- Satisfactory completion of due diligence in all respects to include a Field Examination at Borrower's expense and final credit approval is the sole discretion of Lender.
- All matters related to the legal and borrowing status of the Borrower(s) shall be determined to be entirely satisfactory to Lender and its Legal Counsel to include but not limited to: legally recognized entity in good standing, authority to borrow, satisfactory lien perfection and compliance with all relevant local rules, laws, and regulations.
- Satisfactory review of Borrower's Property, Casualty and Liability Insurance sources and limits.
- Lender shall perform periodic field examinations at Borrower's expense. The scope and frequency of such examinations shall be at Lender's sole discretion.
- Borrower shall open and maintain its principal operating/cash management accounts with lender, which shall include a Lockbox for collection of collateral proceeds that shall be used to pay down the Revolver on a daily basis.
- No material adverse change.
- The negotiation, execution, and delivery of all relevant documentation to include loan and security documentation satisfactory in form and substance to Lender and its counsel.
- Subject to further due diligence, unbilled accounts receivable shall generally be defined as costs actually incurred through performance under prime US Government Contracts (confirmation by US Government that service has been rendered or product delivered) and which will be billed to the Account Debtor within 30 days under billing terms that require payment within a specified period of time and do not require the Borrower to take any additional action to receive payment, e.g. achieve a milestone on the contract.
- All of Lender's due diligence and closing costs paid by Borrower.

Figure 4.1 *(continued)*

Governing Law: Georgia

Important Information about Opening Your New Account and/or Entering
into a Business Relationship with Generic Bank

To help fight the funding of terrorism and money laundering activities, Federal law requires all financial institutions to obtain, verify, and record information that identifies each person or corporation who opens an account and/or enters into a business relationship.

The remainder of this chapter presents some guidelines to consider when seeking early investments and seed capital.

MARKET VALIDATION

Before starting a business and taking capital, validate your products with real customers. Keep in mind that the only market validation anyone cares about is paying customers!

What fundamental, quantifiable market *challenge* did you uncover and create a solution for that moves the buyer beyond the status quo? Alternatively, what quantifiable market *opportunity* did you uncover and create a solution for? The opportunity could be one to build, grow, and scale rather than merely repair.

Exercise 4.3
Industry Dysfunctions or Broken Processes

What are three dysfunctions or broken processes in your industry? What do most of your customers complain about after having dealt with a competitor? What do your customers need to further enhance the value-added products or services they offer *their* customers? Why do you get repeat business and how can you continue to strengthen that position?
Take a minute to capture three:
1. _____
_____
2. _____
_____
3. _____
_____
_____

Savvy entrepreneurs start the prototype of a business to streamline a particular function, process, or administration of a critical service. However, as with most businesses, the plan evolves as the company begins to work with customers to identify their challenges and opportunities along with critical resources they are willing and able to invest in order to address their requirements.

When you bootstrap your formative efforts, it is far easier to be flexible and change directions. The single biggest mistake at this stage is to keep pursuing a market where there is no need for your product or your offering is far ahead of the market requirements. You'll get there, but not before you run out of money! Set aside adequate time to home in on the real and immediate market needs.

Over the next several months and years, you're likely to go through several iterations of the company before crafting a winning formula. It is often a game of trial and error, more trial, more error—and, eventually, success. Again, if you are not tempted by too much early-stage capital, you can retain a healthy stake in the company. The big wins tend to come when several customers show a keen interest in your unique approach. Alternatively, success can be found when the product or service has proven to be successful for others. You need the ability to not only articulate your promised value-proposition but also deliver on it.

Only by quickly responding to market demand—often requiring a revamping of the entire company's focus—can you take advantage of a market opportunity. The results are often greater heights in revenue and profitability, which increase cash flow to appropriate investment efforts.

BOOTSTRAP AND RAISE CAPITAL FOR THE RIGHT REASONS

Seed, bridge, and even friends-and-family money can be "patient capital," which will enable you to be a nimble company during your formative years. If you change direction, you may need additional seed money investors. By staying focused on financial fundamentals such as cash flow, product/project/customer profitability, and consistent investments for a higher-than-average rate of return, you can retire the early debt. However, as you approach a critical mass in revenue, you will realize that the much-needed scale cannot materialize without additional resources and support.

Your early customers might not have minded waiting for support, but new ones expect a technical support call center with 24/7/365 coverage. You could deliver most of the parts inventory with one or two trucks, but now you have more out-of-state clients, which requires a more sophisticated asset management and parts allocation and distribution system. You actually need a human resources department, in-house technology development, and international sales agents.

Even if you don't really feel like you need the money with strong profits and cash on the balance sheet, you will need some "smart" resources. You will need a strong management team beyond your current advisors. A formal board of directors with fiduciary responsibilities will help you grow the company into the $100 million business it can become.

Expanding the business will require more risk. You'll need to diversify the current investment—more than what has gotten you here. Aggressive growth, additional strategic alliance partnerships, and even potential acquisitions (covered in chapter 8) will all require cash. Knowing when to raise capital (and raising it for the right reasons) will be critical to your success.

FIND GOOD PARTNERS TO FUEL YOUR GROWTH

Most savvy entrepreneurs know that their employees can help attract and retain great customers. Beyond them, the next critical "people" decision is that of the right investment partners, with the vested interest to see the business succeed in the long term. Many go at this analysis alone. Others seek out intermediaries such as consultants and investment bankers.

The single most important "value-add" by intermediaries is to *effectively position the company*. In essence, an intermediary can tell the company story and convey the right information to prospective investors. An intermediary can make personal introductions to the most relevant investors. In one situation I know of, an outside consultant became the entrepreneur's vice president of finance and corporate development and a key member of the senior leadership team.

It is critical that you establish options and look at a multitude of sources, from venture capital to private equity to strategic investors. With a polished investor package, you will receive attention from several possible investors—keep in mind, having options becomes very attractive before you narrow the field down to one or two.

At the end of the process, the team will add value as strategic financial partners and board members. A firm that understands how to work closely with bootstrapped companies will be your strongest ally. If they truly understand how bootstrapped businesses operate (as well as your motivation and desire to partner and grow in a smart way), then they will invest the time and effort to advise you and help you scale the business. They will provide resources far beyond capital and make introductions to their portfolio of relationships, which is far more valuable than the initial capital.

NOT IF YOU WANT TO KEEP THEM AS FAMILY AND FRIENDS

Many experts recommend that you raise seed money by asking friends and family to invest. Money borrowed from those closest to you can come with the best low-interest repayment plan you'll ever get. If you are a first-time entrepreneur and not independently wealthy, many institutional investors will not give you capital until you have a paying customer base, possibly making such informal friends-and-family loans necessary. I understand the desire to raise capital from those you know. It is an important element in our sense of community that family and friends take care of each other.

But before accepting their money, *consider the source*, as not all friends and family are created equal, and they all come with strings attached. Some are experienced angels who understand the start-up business world, while others have very little understanding of it. When you take money that puts people at significant risk—because the early stages of a business are simply not very predictable—you have to be careful. This unpredictability also adds an extra level of pressure, which can undermine the execution of the entrepreneur and lead to poor decision making.

When you ask friends and family for a loan, you are appealing to your audience emotionally as much as you are appealing to their rational sense of investing. When you approach people simply because you know them—rather than thinking about what they can contribute besides the liquidity that you need and that they are prepared to give to you for a while—that money isn't very smart capital. Instead, it's money from people who either feel guilty or feel sorry for you or those who think you have integrity and will look after their interests. Seldom does it have anything to do with what that person can contribute other than cash.

As such, buyer beware: capital raised through friends and family can be emotionally draining as you become more and more consumed with not disappointing them and/or inviting more of them into the company than you ever bargained for (read: meddling).

"Never accept money from anyone you might have to sit next to at Thanksgiving dinner," says Tim Knox, serial entrepreneur and bestselling author of the book *Everything I Know About Business I Learned From My Mama*. Tim counsels other entrepreneurs that even if your friends and family are begging you to take their money, think long and hard before accepting.

In many of our discussions with other entrepreneurs who had raised friends-and-family rounds of financing, they concurred that it often led to damaged, even destroyed, relationships. If the business succeeds and they all make back their investment with interest, you are the family hero. But more often than not, you will find yourself sitting at Thanksgiving dinner next to someone whose life savings you lost—and who's not very happy about it. "Did I mention he's holding a rather large carving knife and he keeps referring to you as the turkey?" Tim adds.

If you are fortunate to have friends and family with the wherewithal to get the relationship through the good and very difficult times, you are at a considerable advantage. However, if your business does not produce the promised results, you have the potential to ruin those relationships, because they are more than purely business relationships.

If you do decide to take the capital, it is critical that you set up a repayment schedule in writing and stick to it, so that family gatherings don't become a battleground. You need a very clear plan. For example, "We need $100,000, and it will last us six months, and at the end of ten months, we will have the following...." Have a really good grasp on what that first amount of seed capital will get you, because it will typically take an entrepreneur nine months to get that first round of funding. It is a job unto itself.

On the positive side, if you have friends and family who can support you without putting their financial lives at risk, it is a very encouraging sign to future investors, including the venture capital community. It shows that the commitment goes beyond the entrepreneur having a bad day. It is very encouraging to investors, in particular when the angel investment round includes select friends and family—ideally fewer than five participants. Just keep in mind that friends and family have no place on the board unless they have particular domain experience.

Exercise 4.4
Friends and Family as Sources of Seed Capital

Knowing your friends and family, would you feel comfortable going to them for early stage/seed capital? Would you feel awkward? Would they? If this topic is relevant to you, sit and capture your thoughts on who would you approach, how, and anticipate their responses, objections, and long-term demands of you and the business:

_____
_____
_____
_____

ANGEL INVESTORS

Some entrepreneurs turn to the key individuals I mentioned earlier—often referred to as angel investors—to help seed the business. The term comes from Broadway, where show backers were traditionally known as "angels." Angel investors are usually successful entrepreneurs themselves. Clint Richardson (in his definitive *Growth Company Guide 4.0*)—referred to angel investors as "adventure capitalists." They are typically professionals with money to invest before there is a product or a viable business. Generally, they are most interested in high-risk, high-potential-reward ventures.

Angels are most often friends or business acquaintances with a deeply rooted belief in the entrepreneurial spirit. Most angel investors, especially those who built their own business from the ground up, epitomize the cliché of "been there, done that." They realize the painstaking, labor-of-love effort required to build and grow a business. Most invest only a few times during their lifetime and may not be as sophisticated or rich as the big guns described in the next chapter. Many invest once, lose their money, and never do it again. But angel investors are not only a good source of seed capital. They can also offer a wealth of knowledge and guidance.

Two words of caution, however: In my experience, I have seen several incidents where an angel's investment was poorly documented, poorly structured, and not particularly well considered. Many lack an adequate method for cashing out. Also, angel investors (especially those who are not true entrepreneurs themselves) are not particularly fond of losing their investments. As such, it is critical that you get to know the investor *really* well before accepting his or her money.

The proper fundraising etiquette calls for discreet, quiet research on the angel's investment goals and objectives—as well as that person's style, to ensure it is congruent with yours. You don't want to insult them by asking for a reference of other entrepreneurs in whom they have invested. Entrepreneurs who value the friendship and commitment of their angels will include difficult yet crucial conversations to align the expectations of both the entrepreneur and the investor regarding how the angel can get his or her investment out, well before they accept the investment.

More complex or capital-intensive deals preclude angel financing. According to Larry Bock of Lux Capital, "It all depends on how much money you are actually going to need. If you are eventually going to need $50–100 million, I would go right to a venture investor."

Many entrepreneurs face considerable problems with angel investors and end up spending valuable time and resources manipulating those problems—particularly with investors who overpay—and they establish unrealistic valuations.

Exercise 4.5
Family and Friends as Source of Capital—Part Two

Thinking about your responses from exercise 4.4, how much do you really *like* your family and friends? Do you want your family life invaded—holidays and so forth? Do you want that relationship to rely on your business?

The situation could work out well if they get their money back. And for many early-stage entrepreneurs, they could be your best bet, because oftentimes people who would invest in an early-stage venture are ultimately investing in the person—not the business. So, find some quiet time and answer the following critical questions.

1. Make a prioritized list of five to ten people you would ask to invest in your business. How much would be appropriate to request?

   a. _____
   b. _____
   c. _____
   d. _____
   e. _____
   f. _____
   g. _____
   h. _____
   i. _____
   j. _____

Exercise 4.5 *(continued)*

2. How could you ensure that at least half of the list above would commit the desired amount?

_____

_____

3. How can you put a solid plan in place that commits to repayment with interest?

_____

_____

4. Who else could you include in a small round to broaden the pool beyond immediate friends and family? Think of some potential angels you may have access to.

_____

_____

5. What other critical points would you need to cover with this group to reduce the potential stress and discomfort in the transaction?

_____

_____

_____

BUSINESS INCUBATORS

Another possible resource to accelerate successful development of a new idea or business is an appropriate business incubator. By providing entrepreneurs with a broad base of targeted resources and services—orchestrated by the incubator's management—an incubator's main goal is to "graduate" successful businesses that will leave the program in a self-sustaining mode.

In return, these graduating companies create jobs, commercialize often-academic fledgling ideas and technologies, and strengthen local and regional economies. Many incubators house shared services such as information technology, human resources, administrative and legal support, and often have executives in residence to provide management guidance and to serve as poignant consultants, all of which are very much needed by early-state growing companies.

Many incubators are affiliated with a university, giving entrepreneurs further access to inexpensive office space, university students as interns or co-ops, research assets, and other support services while obtaining early-stage financing to fuel new business growth.

Although many incubation programs focus on technology initiatives, in more recent years new incubators have emerged that target industries as broad and varied as food processing, medical devices, industrial applications (such as space and ceramic technologies), ardent crafts, and software development. Of particular interest are the efforts of a number of incubators that focus on programs support, micro-enterprise creation, and the needs of women and minorities, as well as environmental endeavors.

Note that incubators are typically appropriate for prerevenue or early-stage companies. According to the National Business Incubations Association, there are more than 1,000 incubators in North America, of which 80 percent report providing formal or informal access to capital. Incubators may offer a broad array of financing, which may or may not be appropriate to your business. But for all intents and purposes, both the incubators themselves and the investors they attract are geared toward very early-stage development of product or service ideas.

Getting accepted into an incubator requires completing a screening process to ensure that you meet that incubator's criteria. Most incubator-centric businesses tend to thrive, if by no other means, on a highly concentrated center of entrepreneurial activities—think brown-bag luncheons, proactive collaboration around business or technical issues, pro bono or highly discounted professional services, and so forth. The funds typically available can range from as little as $500 to as much as $25,000 or even more. A good example is the Advanced Technology Development Center in Atlanta at Georgia Tech (see appendix A for more information).

The next chapter will discuss how, with seed capital under your belt or your business already well on its way, you can access the more formal institutional investors. From several state and federal government sources to strategic investors, venture capital, and private equity, the next hurdle is often more challenging and thus less traveled by many entrepreneurs.

Many first-timers are unfamiliar with various protocols and the requirements at each step in the funding process. They are also plagued by misperceptions of a "quick hit." A lot of opportunities are chasing fewer quality funding sources, and the investment community continues to raise the bar on the quality of the businesses as well as of the entrepreneurs and CEOs they are choosing to invest in. One institutional investor shared with me the firm's specific strategy of doing fewer deals but investing deeper in each portfolio company and wider in a particular niche.

In the next chapter, let's take a closer look at the big guns—the power, influence, and sheer size of investment capital from institutional investors.

SUMMARY

☑ Seed capital can come from your own bootstrapping efforts, short-term loans, or individuals who already know and trust you.

☑ Bootstrapping allows the entrepreneur to avoid giving away too much too early in the business's life cycle.

☑ Strong sales and consistent profitability will increase your chances for outside seed capital.

☑ Some of the more uncommon sources of capital include business plan or innovation competitions, grants, supplier financing, SBA loans, and lines of credit.

☑ Next to delivering value for customers, close attention to your financial health and stewardship should be your number-two priority.

☑ Only by quickly responding to market demand—often requiring a revamp of the entire company's focus—can you take advantage of market opportunities.

☑ A polished investor package will help pique the interest of several investment sources.

☑ When you ask friends and family for funding, you are appealing to them emotionally as well as to their rational sense of investing. Be cautious, as not all friends and family are created equal, and they all come with strings attached.

☑ Angels are most often friends or people given warm introductions by business acquaintances and can support both the governance and management of the business.

☑ Business incubators provide entrepreneurs with a broad base of targeted resources and services in an effort to "graduate" successful businesses.

5

Big Guns: Institutional Investors

Raising capital has its own version of the major leagues. Beyond previously discussed bootstrapping and early-stage seed capital, the next stage of the fundraising evolution often requires institutional capital, fueled by sources such as state and federal government, larger corporate entities, or venture capital and private equity firms. These groups not only bring a considerable level of sophistication to the financial stewardship of your company but also heighten operational, process, and personnel performance.

WHAT INSTITUTIONAL INVESTORS LOOK FOR

It is critical that you begin with a certain level of insight as to whether or not your business is right for institutional funding. The following ten-point checklist will be helpful for entrepreneurs to consider.

1. *Core nature of the business.* Unique intellectual property, the opportunity to shape or dominate a market, and the ability to consistently demonstrate well-insulated profit margins are all attributes that attract institutional capital. Of particular interest are value-chain disruptors with the opportunity to reach critical mass. As a general rule, institutional investors love technology investments. Although nontechnology investments are also made—often by private equity firms—there are fewer of them, and they tend to lean toward more traditional financing models.
2. *Shifts in paradigm.* "Me too" products and services will have a very difficult time elevating themselves above the market noise. The more distinctive your business is in how it changes the way consumers embrace and function in a market, the larger will be the initial investment. It is very difficult to raise institutional capital if you start from a position of battling the 800-pound gorilla—unless you have a truly unique approach.
3. *Cash to market.* How much will it cost to develop your idea into a product, the product into a company, and the company into a profitable one? It is no easy feat to accomplish all three. Institutional capital prefers to minimize the cash outlay until the company is capable of reaching profitability with the committed funds.

4. *Path to market.* The more direct your path from concept to reality is, the more attractive the opportunity will be. Institutional investors want to know: Who will buy it? How will they find it? Can others add value to it? These are all critical ingredients. Any opportunity to leverage another company's distribution channel is to your advantage—especially if that company has a vested interest in your success and in keeping that distribution channel open. Proven access to established markets will always be more attractive than entrepreneurs who attempt to invent new distribution channels—which can be extremely costly.

5. *Support cost after the sale.* If your product or service is difficult or complex to assemble, maintain, or transport, or if it requires a multitude of third-party or support infrastructure, that translates into a very high support cost after the sale. Large customer-service organizations, extensive and highly technical training requirements, and complex return or replacement procedures all chip away at margins, making the bottom line that much less attractive.

6. *More about what you keep.* Many entrepreneurs confuse gross revenues with gross margins. Beyond what you actually sell, of particular interest to institutional investors are the margins (sales minus costs) you are able to retain. Significant selling, general, and administrative (SG&A) expenses make it difficult for a company to deliver what is very attractive to institutional investors: high operating or net margins.

7. *Exponential scale.* Can your business generate $100 million to $200 million in profitable growth? As mentioned earlier, ideas by themselves seldom make a product, and products alone seldom make a company. But if you are able to think big, start small, and scale exponentially, the sheer volume—profitably grown—will be of great interest to institutional capital investors.

8. *Strategic value.* Can you build so much value in your business that others are willing to compete to be a part of it, align their brands with it to create strategic partnerships, and even potentially merge with or acquire it?

9. *Global appeal.* Beyond local, regional, and perhaps even national viability or applicability, any time a product or service can overcome geographic boundaries and reach critical mass on a global scale, by definition it quickly outgrows its mom-and-pop perception.

10. *Public market potential.* Even with the recent reporting and compliance challenges of Sarbanes-Oxley, businesses with a portfolio of products and services that can access the public market through an initial public offering (IPO) are attractive to institutional investors, who often get the chance to exit their initial investment with a handsome profit.

The Sarbanes-Oxley Act of 2002 was enacted as U.S. federal law in response to a number of major corporate and accounting scandals including those affecting Enron, Tyco International, Adelphia, Peregrine Systems and WorldCom. These scandals, which cost investors billions of dollars when the share prices of the affected companies collapsed, shook public confidence in the nation's securities markets.

(continued)

The legislation established new or enhanced standards for all U.S. public company boards, management, and public accounting firms. It does not apply to privately held companies. The act contains 11 titles, or sections, ranging from additional corporate board responsibilities to criminal penalties and requires the Securities and Exchange Commission (SEC) to implement rulings on requirements to comply with the new law.

Debate continues over the perceived benefits and costs of SOX. Supporters contend that the legislation was necessary and has played a useful role in restoring public confidence in the nation's capital markets by, among other things, strengthening corporate accounting controls. Opponents of the bill claim that it has reduced America's international competitive edge against foreign financial service providers, claiming that SOX has introduced an overly complex and regulatory environment into U.S. financial markets.

Exercise 5.1
Is Your Business Right for Institutional Investors?

How does your business rate on the above checklist? Below is a "back of the napkin" scorecard on whether your business may be of interest to institutional investors. Keep in mind that this is a rough estimation only and attractiveness of any business to potential investors will vary according to a number of attributes such as available capital in the market, size of the initial and subsequent funding requirements, as well as specific business and industry nuances and key performance metrics.

Give yourself a score of 1–4 on each point:

1. Unique concept/market-dominating potential (1 = not really;   ___
    4 = strong)
2. Unique market approach/value-add (1 = not really; 4 = strong)   ___
3. Cash to market (1 = less than $10 million; 4 = $100+ million)   ___
4. Channels (1 = build your own; 4 = leverage others)   ___
5. Support cost after the sale (1 = high; 4 = low)   ___
6. Gross margins (1 = more than 10 percent; 4 = 50+ percent)   ___
7. Profitable growth (1 = $10 million business; 4 = $100+ million   ___
    business)
8. Strategic value to others (1 = not really; 4 = very high)   ___
9. Global appeal (1 = not really; 4 = strong)   ___
10. IPO potential (1 = not really; 4 = within five years)   ___

Add up your score.

- If you scored less than 15, seek angels and early-stage venture capital.
- 16–30 is a good target for venture capital, some strategic investors, and some smaller private equity firms.
- 30+ is often appealing to private equity and high-profile venture capital firms and bigger, perhaps even international, strategic investors.

If your position is less than desirable with regard to any of these ten points, many institutional capital sources may not present an opportunity for you. A lack of scalability, profitability, or strategic value to others for an eventual exit often tends to be a deal breaker in pursuing institutional capital. Many sources of this type of capital see thousands of proposals each year, and they select to invest in only a handful.

One test of your resilience, persistence, and long-term viability is to pursue government funding.

GOVERNMENT FUNDING

The dawn of government funding can be traced back at least to Queen Isabella of Spain when she decided to fund the voyages of Christopher Columbus. But the ability to get Uncle Sam behind your growing venture today rests on your ability to intelligently navigate an often bureaucratic and complex maze of applications, departments, processes, and the ever-painful and often expensive and draining "waiting game." In case you're wondering, there is no official "small business start-up" pool of nonappropriated funds—but there *are* specific grants focused on very specific needs, which makes government funding an often-talked-about but misunderstood source of business financing.

A number of states and cities have their own targeted grants, as well. For example, the Illinois Recycling Grant Program encourages private organizations to apply for grants that promote diverting recyclable commodities. North Carolina's Division of Pollution Prevention and Environmental Assistance offers several grants, including up to $20,000 in matching funds to develop and implement projects that eliminate or reduce solid waste.

In the Savannah River region of South Carolina and Georgia, entrepreneurs starting tech-based or manufacturing companies can apply for numerous grants. The Small Business Seed Fund for Technical Innovations offers two-year loans of up to $50,000 to support start-ups or business expansions offering new products or improvements to existing ones. Those who successfully complete this grant can apply for an additional two-year grant of up to $250,000 from the Challenge Fund Program for Technology Development.

Two programs in particular operated by the federal government are the Small Business Innovation Research (SBIR) and Small Business Technology Transfer (STTR) programs. The difference between the two programs is that SBIR focuses on innovations and new technologies, while STTR requires a joint focus on a technology transfer between a nonprofit research organization and a commercial business. Both require a tight strategic fit within a framework described by one of several government agencies participating in these programs. A multitude of organizations offer services to help you apply for these grants. Before selecting one, do your due diligence. (To learn more about these organizations, see Appendix A.)

Entrepreneurs across the country often apply for these grants from any of ten federal agencies involved. The stair-step process is comprised of two phases:

- Phase 1: Often earmarked money to finance the development and testing of a prototype in the amount of up to $100,000.
- Phase 2: The commercialization path to take that prototype to the market for amounts of up to $750,000.

Although many applicant businesses clear the phase 1 hurdle, phase 2 becomes considerably more difficult. This iterative process requires patience and clear articulation of the key attributes in the filtering checklist discussed earlier.

Two agencies in particular—the National Institutes of Health (NIH) and the National Science Foundation (NSF)—use a grant system to award money. Other government agencies use the Federal Acquisition Requirement (FAR) process or federal contracting. It is critical to understand that these grants are not lotteries or giveaways, but rather a competitive process to respond to specific needs of these agencies. Each agency often describes its mission and the unique products it will require you to demonstrate congruent with that mission.

One CEO of a supply chain logistics software company I interviewed has had success in the SBIR program not once, but twice. His company was part of an NSF program for two years, and he described it as "extra measured research."

In these programs, 1 percent of the money is allocated to small and medium-size businesses. Each agency must spend that budget through grants, and every agency does it differently. The Department of Defense, for example, supports businesses that focus on defense and military innovations, while the NSF awards grants to companies that are more commerce and transportation oriented.

The process is referred to as a "program solicitation" (see figure 5.1). There is a list of topics each agency will fund. To apply for a grant, send a proposal describing your research in a particular area and the work you intend to do. There is a peer-review group often made up of PhDs and business experts who are very knowledgeable in that specific area. There are also very strict deadlines. Before you extend the effort and resources to apply, you ensure there is clear evidence of a viable fit between your efforts and their particular interest areas and framework.

For their phase 1 proposal, entrepreneurs and their teams may partner with a group of professors at several different universities. There is a strict outline required—forty plus pages, which can take a month of research and writing to complete. After six months of going through the application process, a company can still be turned down for the financing. There are no guarantees. However, the upside is between $100,000 and $150,000 to develop a "proof of concept" (POC) for six months. If your POC is successful, you can then build a proposal for phase 2, which funds $500,000 to $750,000 for two years. This phase requires a much more extensive 100-page application, which is essentially the commercialization plan for your product. Those who have reached this milestone describe this phase as being three times the work of the other and heavily focused on building a prototype.

Figure 5.1
Sample NSF Program Solicitation

Small Business Innovation Research and Small Business Technology Transfer Programs Phase I Solicitation FY-2008 (SBIR/STTR)

Program Solicitation
NSF 07-586

Replaces Document(s):
NSF 07-551

 National Science Foundation

Directorate for Engineering
    Industrial Innovation and Partnerships

Full Proposal Deadline(s) (due by 5 p.m. proposer's local time):

December 04, 2007

Topic: Emerging Opportunities (EO) – encompasses 3 very broad subtopics: Bio & Environmental Technologies (BE); Components & Systems (CS); Software & Services (SS) – Do not submit proposals prior to November 4, 2007

REVISION NOTES

Proposals not meeting administrative requirements are not accepted by the SBIR program. The following list highlights key administrative reasons for return without review:

- A proposal submitted after 5:00 P.M. (proposer's/submitter's time local time) on the deadline date. The "Proposer" is the company and the time zone associated with the company's address will be used to determine if a proposal is late.*
- A Project Summary without all required information (reference section A.9.2).
- A Project Description that exceeds 15 pages and does not have all parts.
- An SBIR proposal with a budget exceeding $100,000 or an STTR proposal with a budget exceeding $150,000.
- A proposal missing a Company Commercialization History; if the company has certified that it has received previous SBIR/STTR Phase II awards (reference section A.9.9.2).
- A proposal that has documents placed in the "Additional Single Copy Documents" module in FastLane.
- Collaborative proposals (defined as simultaneous proposal submissions from different organizations, with each organization requesting a separate award). Note:

(continued)

Figure 5.1 (*continued*)

Small business concerns are encouraged to collaborate with research institutions; however, only one proposal should result.

SUMMARY OF PROGRAM REQUIREMENTS

General Information

Program Title:

Small Business Innovation Research and Small Business Technology Transfer Programs Phase I Solicitation FY-2008 (SBIR/STTR)

Synopsis of Program:

The SBIR/STTR Programs stimulate technological innovation in the private sector by strengthening the role of small business concerns in meeting Federal research and development needs, increasing the commercial application of federally supported research results, and fostering and encouraging participation by socially and economically disadvantaged and women-owned small businesses.

The significant difference between the SBIR and STTR programs is that STTR requires researchers at universities and other research institutions to play a significant intellectual role in the conduct of each STTR project. These university-based researchers, by joining forces with a small company, can spin-off their commercially promising ideas while they remain primarily employed at the research institution.

Cognizant Program Officer(s):

- Thomas Allnutt, SBIR/STTR Biotechnology Program Director, telephone: (703) 292-5332, email: tallnutt@nsf.gov
- Errol Arkilic, SBIR/STTR Information Technology/Emerging Opportunities Program Director, telephone: (703) 292-8095, email: earkilic@nsf.gov
- Muralidharan Nair, SBIR/STTR Electronics Program Director, telephone: (703) 292-7059, email: mnair@nsf.gov

Applicable Catalog of Federal Domestic Assistance (CFDA) Number(s):

- 47.041 — Engineering

Award Information

Anticipated Type of Award: Other Grant Fixed Amount Awards

Estimated Number of Awards: 150 awards of which approximately 125 will be SBIR Phase I awards and approximately 25 will be STTR Phase I awards (pending availability of funds).

Anticipated Funding Amount: $16,250,000 with approximately $12,500,000 for SBIR Phase I and approximately $3,750,000 and STTR Phase I (pending the availability of funds). A total of $16.5 million for this solicitation.

Eligibility Information

Organization Limit:

Proposals may only be submitted by the following:

- For-profit organizations: U.S. commercial organizations, especially small businesses with strong capabilities in scientific or engineering research or education.

(continued)

Figure 5.1 (*continued*)

PI Limit:

The primary employment of the Principal Investigator (PI) must be with the small business concern at the time of the award. A PI must spend a minimum of one calendar month of an SBIR Phase I project and a minimum of two calendar months on an STTR Phase I project. Employment releases and certifications of intent shall be required prior to award.

Limit on Number of Proposals per Organization: 4

Limit on Number of Proposals per PI: None Specified

Proposal Preparation and Submission Instructions

A. Proposal Preparation Instructions
- **Letters of Intent:** Not Applicable
- **Full Proposal Preparation Instructions:** This solicitation contains information that supplements the standard Grant Proposal Guide (GPG) proposal preparation guidelines. Please see the full text of this solicitation for further information.

B. Budgetary Information
- **Cost Sharing Requirements:** Cost Sharing is not required by NSF.
- **Indirect Cost (F&A) Limitations:** Indirect costs, inclusive of fringe benefits, are limited to an effective rate of 150% of direct salaries and wages. (See Section V.A.9.6)
- **Other Budgetary Limitations:** Other budgetary limitations apply. Please see the full text of this solicitation for further information.

C. Due Dates
- **Full Proposal Deadline(s)** (due by 5 P.M. proposer's local time):

  December 04, 2007

  Topic: Emerging Opportunities (EO)—encompasses 3 very broad subtopics: Bio & Environmental Technologies (BE); Components & Systems (CS); Software & Services (SS)—Do not submit proposals prior to November 4, 2007

Proposal Review Information Criteria

Merit Review Criteria: National Science Board approved criteria. Additional merit review considerations apply. Please see the full text of this solicitation for further information.

Award Administration Information

Award Conditions: Additional award conditions apply. Please see the full text of this solicitation for further information.

Reporting Requirements: Additional reporting requirements apply. Please see the full text of this solicitation for further information.

(*continued*)

Figure 5.1 (*continued*)

TABLE OF CONTENTS

Summary of Program Requirements

I. **Introduction**
II. **Program Description**
III. **Award Information**
IV. **Eligibility Information**
V. **Proposal Preparation and Submission Instructions**

    A. Proposal Preparation Instructions
    B. Budgetary Information
    C. Due Dates
    D. FastLane Requirements

VI. **NSF Proposal Processing and Review Procedures**

    A. NSF Merit Review Criteria
    B. Review and Selection Process

VII. **Award Administration Information**

    A. Notification of the Award
    B. Award Conditions
    C. Reporting Requirements

VIII. **Agency Contacts**
IX. **Other Information**

STRATEGIC INVESTORS

Another interesting avenue to getting your business funded is through a strategic investor. These investors can be multibillion-dollar companies or individual investors who add significant value through deep and often unique industry insights or through their portfolio of strategic relationships, which are vital in the early stages of a growing company.

It is important to understand that strategic investors are operating firms—often conglomerates—that invest in other operating companies. UPS, for example, has a Strategic Enterprise Fund, which is, in essence, a corporate venture group focused on developing critical partnerships in the emerging technology space, usually with companies that are relevant to their interests of supply chain and asset management.

Strategic investment is a particularly valuable asset, because almost any type of business partnership that could result in a stake in your company would give the investor a stronger incentive to help you. The investment division of a large corporation is often called a corporate venture capital (CVC) arm. Perhaps the most notable CVC group is the Intel Capital Fund, which has reportedly invested more than $7.5 billion in an estimated 1,000 companies since 1991, including a notable transaction in Research in Motion (RIM), the parent company of BlackBerry.

Some companies don't have CVC arms, making it particularly difficult to identify the right person to approach about making a strategic investment in your business. Others, such as IBM or Cardinal Health, avoid strategic investments altogether. Sample companies that do participate in corporate-related venture activities include Hitachi (Hitachi Corporate Venture Catalyst Division), Intel (Intel Capital Fund), Panasonic (Panasonic Digital Concepts Center), Siemens (Siemens Venture Capital), Kodak (Kodak Venture Relations), T-Mobile (T-Mobile Venture Fund), Chevron (Chevron Technologies Ventures), Nokia (Nokia Growth Partners), and Motorola (Motorola Ventures). More information about these and other resources can be found in the Venture Capital section of appendix A, where you will also find information about the National Venture Capital Association website and its current members.

There are a multitude of reasons for making strategic investments, and financial gain may not always be a top priority, unlike the aims of traditional institutional investors. Because many early-stage entrepreneurial ventures tend to be particularly nimble and innovative, CVC divisions will often make strategic investments just to get an early glimpse of new technologies or a potential expansion of current initiatives in a particular vertical or niche market. One interesting example is Nokia Growth Partners, which focuses on opportunities in "mobility, communications, and the Internet." Some of its investments have supported a video system for social networks and mobile phones (kyte.tv), mobile graphics (Morpho, Inc.), and electronic payments (ViVOtech). Likewise, in the pharmaceuticals industry, Merck and Pfizer consistently make strategic investments in biotech companies in an effort to maintain a healthy pipeline of new drugs.

Many strategic investments are a minority stake and part of what is referred to as a *syndicate*—a group of like-minded investors, typically venture capitalists. Often the investments are made in businesses that are beyond the early or seed stage. The syndicate provides credibility by association. It is typically very difficult for a small company to sell to marquee customers, but the syndicate can help the entrepreneur develop a succinct go-to-market strategy. It can also help ensure critical deliverables at key incremental stages. The strategic investors within the syndicate can help by making introductions to its own prime customer base.

Another strong asset in the strategic investment process is the validation of a new technology, process, or approach. One interesting example is the company INSIDE Contactless—funded by Samsung Ventures America, Nokia Growth Partners, and Motorola Ventures—which develops microprocessors for near-field communication.

Yet another key value of strategic investments is that investors often provide access to a considerably broader base of expertise. Intel Capital, for example, regularly holds global events and workshops for its portfolio companies, giving them considerable early access to future technologies and invaluable product roadmaps.

The drawback to strategic investors, on the other hand, is that the person or team who makes the initial investment decision can be very different from the operating business assigned to work with the entrepreneur, creating the potential for misaligned incentives. The other main pitfall is that, unlike financial investors, strategic investors can shift their corporate investment strategy for no particular reason, and if that investment philosophy changes, you could lose support in financing future rounds through no fault of your own.

One more critical aspect of strategic investors is the competitive landscape. If, for example, the Coca-Cola Company backs you, you might as well forget about doing business with PepsiCo or other competing beverage firms. And if your solution is specifically for the beverage industry, that will make any other potential exits very difficult.

One of the biggest fears of many entrepreneurs when it comes to strategic investors is that a bigger, well-capitalized investor will steal their intellectual property (IP). This is largely because the intricate details of sharing the small company's confidential information oftentimes becomes somewhat murky. A strategic investor could take your valuable concepts and walk away after the initial round. This fear legitimizes the need for a thorough review of your IP documentation and protection filing process and the support of top-notch, credible law firms to construct solid confidentiality agreements.

Although the number of strategic investment deals is currently less than in 2000 (down by more than 50 percent), the deals that *are* getting done tend to be more definitive of their strategic and less opportunistic nature. This trend argues for addressing my earlier comments about better aligning a corporate champion from the product or business group with the investment in your company to act or serve as an internal sponsor.

DEALING WITH STRATEGIC INVESTORS

Here are five things you should consider when dealing with a strategic investor:

1. *Revenue mindset:* The best strategic investments generate revenue from untapped markets or niche opportunities for both your business and your strategic partners.
2. *Eyes wide open:* Strategic investors have been known to create nonstandard venture capital terms such as right of first refusal and exclusivity. Keep in mind that exclusivity isn't necessarily evil. In the pharmaceutical industry, for example, it's often expected that if Merck or Pfizer open their global distribution to you, it will guarantee very solid and profitable market coverage for your business. However, the right of first refusal for an acquisition could reduce the valuation of a potential sale, as competitors won't be able to make offers for your business.

3. *No exit strategy:* Competitors to the strategic investor will seldom want to partner with you, limiting your exit opportunities.
4. *Past performance:* Do your due diligence. What successes has this strategic partner had with other investments, and what are their internal and external sources of influence to get things done?
5. *Aligned expectations:* Clear, consistent communication is the only avenue to set and retain aligned expectations.

Exercise 5.2
Is a Strategic Investor Right for Your Business?

Is a strategic investor or corporate venture capital (CVC) group right for your business? Here are five questions to answer, often asked by the due-diligence teams of these groups:

1. Are you a niche player focused on a unique and "upside" potential value to a larger global organization?

2. How strong is your competitive landscape for similar functionality, and where are you compared to their development and go-to-market cycle?

3. What does the build-versus-buy decision tree look like for a potential strategic investor? Given their vast resources, is there a reason they wouldn't throw sufficient resources at the problem your solution offers and build it themselves rather than partner or invest in your company?

4. Is your intellectual property sufficiently documented and legally protected?

5. Who are some potential strategic investors or CVC groups you could approach, and what's the brief introductory paragraph you would use to get their attention?

Can you think of three to five individuals who could make these introductions?
a. _____
b. _____
c. _____
d. _____
e. _____

Strategic investments can be extremely beneficial, particularly when in need of capturing a new market. They will require an extensive amount of communication, planning, and investment of time and effort, but this investment can ultimately produce a great deal of long-term value for your business.

Now let's take a closer look at traditional venture capital.

VENTURE CAPITAL

If you run a high-growth business able to generate at least $15 million in revenue in the next three to five years, institutional venture capital (VC) may be a good choice. VC money comes from professionally managed funds predominantly aimed at financing a proven product or service from development through expansion to maturity. Endorsements from successful, branded VC firms (those who are committed to this type of high-risk/high-potential-reward investing) certainly put you on the map as a disciplined business venture that is more likely to succeed.

Despite cyclical downturns in the periods between 1989 and 1992 and between 2000 and 2004, the VC community has enjoyed unprecedented amounts of high-profile publicity for both its firms and their portfolio entrepreneurs. VC investors are accustomed to the hiccups of the process and can anticipate and often prevent them. Many times, they can prevent CEOs from making mistakes previously made by other portfolio company leaders. In a company's growth stage, the entrepreneur can benefit a great deal from an experienced venture capitalist.

VC is highly motivated by market euphoria ("buzz"). In the very early stages of traditional technology companies, many entrepreneurs are steadfastly focused on viral marketing—getting their messages out through word of mouth, blogs, and independent recommendations by others, on- or offline. This often-informal underground circulation of news of frequently inflated proportions leads to an enhanced perception of the business's potential. To illustrate this point, let's take a look at the Gartner Hype Cycle (see figure 5.2).

This type of graphic representation of the maturity adoption and business applications of new technologies has been around since the mid-1990s. Gartner, Inc., even uses hype cycles to illustrate the overenthusiasm for "hype" and consistent subsequent disappointment with the introduction of the next trendy mousetrap. The hype cycle graph depicts how a particular technology typically moves through five sequential stages:

- Stage 1, "Technology Trigger": A breakthrough, product launch, or other type of event creates a significant amount of press and volcanic interest.
- Stage 2, "Peak of Inflated Expectations": A frenzy of publicity, fueled by enthusiasm and unrealistic expectations, masks a disproportionate number of failures relative to quantifiable success stories.

- Stage 3, "Trough of Disillusionment": Failure to meet the hyped expectations makes the technology unfashionable, which leads to its abandonment by the media.
- Stage 4, "Slope of Enlightenment": Practical applications of the technology, often considerable deviations from its original intent, come to fruition.
- Stage 5, "Plateau of Productivity": Critical benefits become widely accepted. Stability of second and third generations creates very real sustainable advantages in either broad-based appeal (horizontal) or key niche markets (vertical).

Ed Sim, in his *BeyondVC* blog (www.beyondvc.com), references a start-up cycle illustrating early phases for building and scaling a business, as opposed to an early exit or flip. The hard work is in maintaining, if not optimizing, performance after reaching the downslope of the bell curve of the heaviest buzz and the final revelation of the company's real future (as illustrated in figure 5.3). Of particular interest is Sim's illustration of a home run, double, single, or groundout.

Venture capital is typically money invested in private businesses at a high risk for potentially high rewards. Many of those companies may have outgrown traditional sources such as commercial banks or factoring (a form

Figure 5.2
Sample Gartner Hype Cycle for Emerging Technologies

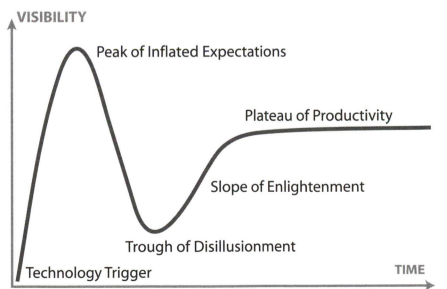

Source: Wikipedia, image created by Jeremy Kemp. http://en.wikipedia.org/wiki/Image: Gartner_Hype_Cycle.svg.

Figure 5.3
Ed Sim's Beyond VC Start-up Cycle

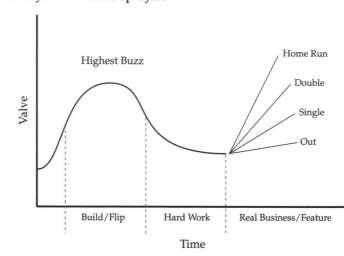

of receivables financing where the factor/lender pays you a discounted portion of your accounts receivable and collects them from your customers when they become due) or deem funding from those sources as inappropriate for the scale of their growth. Often, a VC investor acquires a minority interest with highly liquid equity using a variety of financial structures and contractual agreements to ensure their participation at a board level, thus gaining direct access to information about a company's performance. Driven by the desire to generate a strong rate of return for their invested capital, VC firms typically search for companies with the ability to generate very rapid growth (some call this "hypergrowth"). Turnarounds and leveraged buyouts are also viable prospects for venture capitalists.

VC deal structures vary from deal to deal. Below are some critical things to consider:

- *Security type.* VC firms typically prefer a convertible preferred stock, which gives them advantages over other stockholders. Shares are typically convertible into common stock, which is mandatory if the company goes public.
- *Pricing and valuation.* The amount invested and number of shares of stock determines the value of the company. Investors typically acquire a percentage of the business's fully diluted stock ownership for a given amount. What is often referred to as a *term sheet*, for example, could outline that a VC group will invest $2 million to purchase one million

shares of convertible preferred stock, representing 25 percent of the company's capital stock after the investment. In this scenario, the company's valuation would be set at $6 million premoney and $8 million postmoney.

- *Full disclosure.* VC companies prepare extremely detailed agreements and disclosure schedules—ten or twenty single-spaced pages would not be unusual.
- *Liquidation and dividend.* VC firms also devise in their agreements a purchase preference that entitles them to a predetermined amount if the company is ever liquidated. The preferred status of their equity position typically translates into their investment plus a predetermined return in advance of dividends to common stockholders.
- *Antidilution clauses.* To protect their consistent percentage of the company's stock, these rights entitle investors to receive additional shares if the company should sell its stock for a lower price after the initial VC buy-in. *Ratchet antidilution* and *weighted-average antidilution* provisions are formulas to guard against loss of that equity's value.
- *Voting rights.* VC agreements almost always include the right to elect one or more seats on the company's board of directors and the right to approve certain types of amendments to the company's charter, the sale of the business, or any issuance of new securities.
- *Preemptive rights.* Because of their preferred stock position, venture capitalists also retain the right to buy stock in future rounds of a company's funding efforts.
- *Vesting agreements.* More aggressive VC companies tend to negotiate the shares of the founders and management, subject to a vesting schedule, so that they will forfeit their shares or their stock if they leave the company.
- *Management noncompetes.* The founders and management of the company are typically required to sign a noncompete agreement that states they will focus exclusively on the vested business and protect confidential trade secrets.

There are a number of other possible clauses, as well. The savvy entrepreneur would be well served to invest in a credible, highly experienced law firm with strong acumen in navigating these often complex venture capital agreements.

As previously mentioned, I found the website www.thefunded.com particularly helpful when evaluating possible VC options, yet most entrepreneurs that raise VC funding agreed that by far the most effective form of due diligence was through informal conversations with CEOs who had worked with particular firms and their partners.

Take a look at exercise 5.3. Did you notice that none of the questions have anything to do with the actual investment of capital? That's because many of the VC investments that are deemed successful, as well as those either side would call a failure, happen more because of the chemistry between the parties involved than the actual financial transaction.

Exercise 5.3
Venture Capital in Your Business

So you think you want to invite venture capitalists into your business? The best recommendation I can give you is to find one of thousands of entrepreneurs who have traveled down this path during the past year and ask them these simple questions:

1. What was it like to have a venture capitalist on your board?

_____

_____

2. What were some of the areas of conflict?

_____

_____

3. Were they macro- or micromanagers?

_____

_____

4. How would you describe their style as a board member?

_____

_____

5. Did you have good chemistry?

_____

_____

6. Was there respect, collaboration, and a supportive decision-making process?

_____

_____

_____

You don't necessarily have to *like* your investors, but you do have to respect and trust them. Likewise, any astute VC company taking on a great deal of risk must possess a high opinion of the target business's CEO—in terms of vision, business acumen, character, and so on. "My opinion of the CEO far outweighs any of the other components when deciding whether or not to invest," says Cate Cavanaugh Krensavage, managing partner of Palo Alto Capital Partners.

Most members of the capital community will agree that, by far, their most successful access—and often competition for quality entrepreneurs and deals—is through their portfolio of functional and strategic relationships. "Deal flow," as it is commonly referred to, is a VC firm's widely cast net into the professional services community. Deal flow is generated through relationships with colleagues or friends of existing portfolio companies and executives, as well as through traditional research and academic circles. These relationships serve to help the venture capitalist search for investment-worthy opportunities. As such, an entrepreneur's best bet is to follow these five search strategies to begin narrowing the field to the most appropriate VC investors.

1. *Industry Vertical.* Many VC firms have come to realize that they cannot maintain a high level of intellectual horsepower in a multitude of industries. As such, an accelerated trend is that of vertical integration. A focus on a particular technology, industry, or business enables the investors to identify early performers as well as high potentials. Specialization by VC companies allows you as the entrepreneur to target parties that should be highly interested and to filter out irrelevant ones. But a word of caution: Don't expect to bluff these specialists, as they are likely to either possess a great deal of expertise themselves or have access to astute subject matter experts. They also have the resources to engage world-renowned experts to fret out your hypothesis or critical assumptions.

2. *Geographic Preference.* As many VC investors tend to be fairly hands-on, geographic limitations will become a factor. From frequent board meetings to helping the portfolio company stay focused on a product development roadmap, having to spend hours on a plane traveling thousands of miles is simply not attractive. As such, many venture capitalists have developed geographic prejudices, which also allow them to be intimately familiar with early-stage sparks of interesting ideas in that area.

3. *Stage of Company's Maturity.* Similar to an industry or geographic focus, many VC firms also have developed a very strong bias toward varying stages of a company's life cycle. Many prefer to invest in the early stages—often referred to as pre- or "A" rounds, which constitute a company's initial series of institutional funding—while others favor the more mature stages. This is a very logical approach, as the investors quickly develop a feel for where and how they choose to care for companies' nurturing requirements at varying stages.

4. *Lead Status.* In a syndicate of multiple VC firms, there are typically lead investors with deep domain expertise and extensive due-diligence capabilities, and then there are "follow-on" investors, who are considerably less active, tending to go along with the lead firms. Often, the lead firm's presence alone attracts other investors more typical of second, third, fourth, and subsequent rounds of venture funding.

5. *Deal Size.* Most VC investors will have an ideal size of investment and duration or lifetime of that investment in mind for any given company. This range limit is predicated by the size of the fund that the VC firm is managing. For example, $250 million to $1 billion funds seldom look at $1 million investments.

PRIVATE EQUITY

Institutional investors are often organizations with large sums of money to invest, such as banks, insurance companies, pension funds, hedge funds,

Figure 5.4
Typical Private Equity Structure

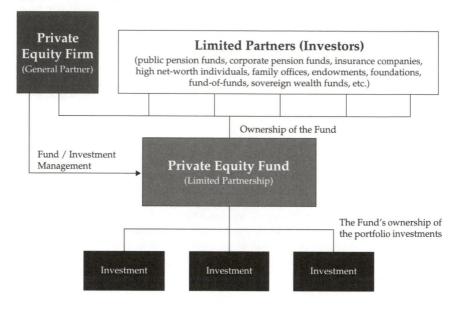

and mutual funds. Institutional investors provide private equity capital to create a risk-tolerant return exceeding that which could be obtained in public markets. Private equity groups (PEGs) become the vehicle by which these institutional investors invest in privately held companies.

Certain very large institutional investors (often called *limited partners*) have the critical mass to create a very diversified portfolio of private equity funds (see figure 5.4). Another strategy is to diversify asset holdings through investments in a "fund of funds"—private equity funds that invest in *other* private equity funds to minimize investment risk by spreading the exposure through a large number of investment vehicles, with different types and regional foci.

PEGs typically receive a return on their investment through various means:

- Sale of the company to another private equity firm
- A merger or acquisition of their private companies
- An Initial Public Offering (IPO)—that is, sale of that private company to the public market
- Recapitalization, by which, through raising debt or generating cash flow, the PEG receives distributed cash

One of the key differences between traditional venture capital and private equity financing is that private equity firms typically invest in considerably more mature "old economy" businesses such as food, transportation, manufacturing, and distribution. For example, Atlanta-based Arcapita (backed by the Bahrain-based Islamic Bank) has strong equity positions in a portfolio of assets ranging from Sirius Airplanes to Loehmann's retail stores and Caribou Coffee.

Additionally, most private equity investments take a majority stake or controlling position in their portfolio companies. Due to the sheer size of most private equity investments, they tend to focus more on a "buy and hold" strategy. Private equity investors typically hold investments over a ten- to fifteen-year span, compared to the three- to five-year investment horizon of a venture capital firm with limited exit options.

Finally, although private equity is generally more risk averse than venture capital, private equity continues to provide a higher return to its funding partners than other traditional assets, such as public equity and bonds.

A very broad base of styles and types of private equity exist globally, of which venture capital and leveraged buyouts (LBO) are the most common. Venture capital has already been discussed. LBOs refer to the strategy of acquiring a company, business unit, or noncore asset through heavy utilization of financial leverage (loans or other funding). In the late 1980s, this type of financial engineering reached historic heights when Kohlberg Kravis Roberts (better known as KKR) closed a $31.1 billion takeover of RJR Nabisco. A combination of decreasing interest rates, looser lending standards, and regulatory changes for publicly traded companies set the stage for the largest boom period that the private equity market has seen, between 2005 and 2007. Toys R Us, the Hertz Corporation, Metro-Goldwyn-Mayer (MGM), Sunguard, HCA, and Chrysler are all examples of megabuyouts.

By July 2007, the turmoil in the mortgage market had spilled over into the leveraged finance and high-yield debt markets, causing a noticeable slowdown in additional plans for large private equity deals. This tumult is characterized by the following interesting facts:

- The five biggest private equity deals to date involved more money than the annual budgets of either Russia or India.
- The annual revenue of the largest private equity firms and their portfolio companies would give private equity four of the top twenty-five spots in the *Fortune* 500 (see figure 5.5).
- The top twenty private equity firms control companies that employ an estimated 4.5 million workers.

One of the most interesting aspects of the private equity industry is that the most profitable deals typically get done during times of market turmoil. The current market has many large buyout deals stuck in financing gridlock, and new deal announcements are at an unprecedented industry standstill. Even with an increased cost of debt, smaller-scale global opportunities can provide very attractive multiples (a shorthand

Table 5.1
Private Equity International Top 10 Global Private Equity Firms

Rank	Firm	Headquarters	Capital raised as of 2007 (billions)
1	The Carlyle Group	Washington, DC	$32.50
2	Kohlberg Kravis Roberts	New York	$31.10
3	Goldman Sachs Principal Investment Area	New York	$31.00
4	The Blackstone Group	New York	$28.36
5	TPG Capital	Fort Worth	$23.50
6	Permira	London	$21.47
7	Apax Partners	London	$18.85
8	Bain Capital	Boston	$17.30
9	Providence Equity Partners	Providence, RI	$16.36
10	CVC Capital Partners	London	$15.65

term referring to how much an interested investor will pay per dollar of earnings).

Here are three reasons for the recent surge in private equity activity:

1. Shares of many public companies have been relatively inexpensive when compared to the value of their assets and revenues generated.
2. Capital from limited partners available to private equity firms has increased as more pension funds and foundations allocate more of their portfolio to private equity.
3. The global market for debt, which is borrowed to "financially engineer" these acquisitions, has remained consistent.

Private Equity Myths and Misconceptions

According to the Private Equity Council, there are many myths and misconceptions about what private equity is and isn't. Let's review a few:

Myth: *Private equity and hedge funds are the same.* Private equity invests in companies with the intention to develop and operate them for several years. Hedge funds are a loosely defined category of investment pools—similar to mutual funds—that invest in publicly traded companies, currencies, or commodities.

Myth: Private equity investors are predominantly wealthy individuals. Public pension funds, university endowments, and foundations make up the single largest group, accounting for a third of all capital allocated to private equity. Other investors are large corporate funds.

Myth: Private equity firms have no commitment to growing companies. The private equity business model relies heavily on investing in and strengthening undervalued companies, making them worth considerably more when they are sold to another buyer or the public market.

Myth: Private equity firms are quick to flip companies for a buck. Most private equity firms are long-term investors, because it takes time to substantially enhance earnings and cash flow and thus make the portfolio companies more attractive to future buyers.

Myth: Private equity firms weaken portfolio companies by stripping their assets. Buying a company and selling off its parts—commonly referred to as *asset stripping*—is inherently risky, as many operating companies are difficult to dissect without risking collapse.

Myth: Private equity buyouts typically result in layoffs. Although some reorganization may be necessary, long-term job growth is more often the case, at a much faster pace compared to traditionally financed firms.

Myth: Private equity firms load up companies they buy with massive amounts of debt. The optimal capital structure for a potential acquisition is typically comprised of multiple investors investing their own equity and thus making prudent investments, not highly speculative ones.

Myth: Pension fund investments in private equity endanger the retirement security of tens of millions of Americans. Pension funds often have a strict limit in their governance models that can be allocated to private equity—less than 10 percent.

Myth: Private equity firms operate in a secretive and closed environment. Limited partners often know more about their private equity investments than average investors know about their 401(k) plans. Private equity portfolio companies that issue public debt must file a 10-K report with the Securities and Exchange Commission.

Myth: When public companies go private, conflicts of interest create a less-than-stellar price for shareholders. Private equity transactions for a public company are very similar to a merger, in which the board and shareholders vote on a price per share.

What Do Private Equity Firms Look for When Investing?

First and foremost, private equity firms look for a platform when they invest. For example, Chrysler is not just one car; it is a portfolio of vehicles that matches a very broad base of tastes, preferences, and capabilities; furthermore, the company enhances its platform with financing options such as Chrysler Credit and an extensive service department. Dunkin' Donuts isn't just pastries; it's also a real estate play. First Data, a recent KKR acquisition with a market value of an estimated $30 billion, is more than just payment processing; it's a platform to transform innovation in mobile transactions (imagine paying for your next vending machine soft drink with your cell phone).

Another feature private equity firms like to see is cash flow. As mentioned earlier, strong revenue performance and consistent cash-flow generation give a company the flexibility to create a multitude of options with that cash.

Exercise 5.4
What Private Equity Investors Look For

What are the critical attributes private equity investors generally consider before making an investment? Here are the top ten. See how your business fits the bill.

1. Strong sustained growth (e.g., Caribou Coffee exponentially increasing its number of retail coffee shops)
2. A business model not specifically tied to commodity prices
3. An operation that provides a niche product or service (e.g., Sirius Airplanes targeting the air taxi market)
4. A simple, easy-to-understand business
5. Opportunities to generate higher revenues through organic growth, as well as via acquisitions
6. A battle-tested, seasoned management team
7. The ability to sustain margins, ideally even during economic downturns
8. A diverse and noncyclical customer base
9. Current shareholders willing to part with some equity for a bigger bite of the apple
10. An ability to return an attractive multiple with enhanced market position

Other characteristics private equity firms look for are listed in exercise 5.4. In the last item listed, the term *multiple*, as noted earlier, refers to some aspect of a company's performance measure to show how much an interested investor will pay per dollar of earnings. A profit-to-earnings (PE) ratio of 10 means that a $20 share of stock earns $2 (earnings per share, or EPS). Investors of this company would therefore be willing to pay a multiple of 10—ten times the current earning per share of the stock.

Private Equity's Contribution to the Global Economy

The past few years have been unlike any in private equity's history. Between 1991 and 2006, private equity firms worldwide returned more than $430 billion in profit to limited partner investors, according to research firm Private Equity Intelligence. During the fifteen years from 1980 to 2005, the top quartile of private equity firms generated annualized returns to investors of 39.1 percent. By contrast, the Standard & Poor's 500 returned 12.3 percent a year during the same period. This means that $1,000, continuously invested with these firms during that period, would have generated $3.8 million in value compared to $18,200 from the public market.

As the spotlight on megafunds and megadeals pulls away from the sector, some fundamental questions remain:

- Will large deals such as Chrysler or First Data pay off in the long run?
- Will limited partners see a significant return on investment in such megafunds?

- With more costly and limited debt, what challenges lie ahead for firms attempting to continue to invest in their large portfolio companies?
- What fundamental shifts in mind-set will the private equity industry have to absorb?
- Will limited partners pull back or lean toward smaller buyout funds?
- Will U.S. private equity firms soon be overshadowed by European and Asian firms, as well as sovereign wealth vehicles such as Dubai Holdings?
- And most critical, will the exit environment realign with the expected returns from this industry?

SUMMARY

☑ Institutional capital such as state and federal government agencies, larger corporate entities, and venture capital or private equity funds bring a considerable level of sophistication to the financial stewardship of any company as they demand heightened operational, process, and personnel performance.

☑ Institutional investors look for unique intellectual property or market approaches with accelerated cash and channels to market, controlled support cost after the sale, providing strong gross margins and consistent profitable growth with global appeal.

☑ Institutional investors' ideal exit from an investment is a sale to a strategic investor or another institutional investor or access to the public market (IPO).

☑ Federal government programs provide unique access to agency funding intended to transfer innovations and new technologies between nonprofit research organizations and commercial businesses.

☑ Strategic investors, often the venture arms of multibillion-dollar conglomerates, tend to invest in developing critical partnerships in the emerging technology space with companies that are relevant to their market interests.

☑ High-growth businesses able to generate at least $15 million in revenue in the next three to five years are likely to attract institutional venture capital— professionally managed funds predominantly aimed at financing product development all the way to expansion capital.

☑ Venture capital investments, especially from syndicates, include extensive legal and structural details, so engaging the support of professional legal and accounting services is critical.

☑ Private equity funds, supported by large institutional pension funds, insurance companies, private investment groups, and banks (limited partners), tend to invest in more mature industries, take a majority stake position, and hold a portfolio company for a longer period of time than venture capitalists.

6

Avenues for Alternative Capital

What if your business doesn't lend itself to the key attributes sought after by institutional investors? Perhaps you are not likely to hit $100 million in revenue or develop the next sexy biotech solution—and furthermore, you are not looking to give away a majority stake in your company.

As many entrepreneurs have experienced, even in the most perilous economic situations—personally borrowing from credit cards to meet payrolls or begging key suppliers for forgiveness in delayed payables, for example—there are alternative sources and access to creative capital that are often ignored. This chapter discusses just a few.

LEASING

Some of the largest needs for financing are often around access to equipment, machinery, and other physical assets needed to undertake a business initiative. According to the Equipment Leasing Association (ELA), an estimated 80 percent of U.S. companies lease some or all of their equipment requirements. As a dominant tool to fuel growth, the flexibility, practicality, and cost-effectiveness of leasing can often improve financial results by stabilizing cash flow and capital budgets.

Whether you struggle with inconsistent cash flow, limited or no investment capital for fixed assets, bank credit line restrictions, or in the case of the tech world, equipment that becomes obsolete in a couple of years, leasing allows for a more concentrated focus on the productive use of equipment without the potential risks of owning it. Take particular care to structure leases correctly to maximize tax advantages, which will allow you to deduct lease payments as a business expense rather than depreciate them as an asset.

Some benefits to leasing include:

- *All-inclusiveness.* Leasing can provide 100 percent financing, to include such things as software, hardware, consulting, maintenance, freight, installation, and even training costs—all "soft costs" associated with equipment purchases.

- *Working capital conservation.* By minimizing the initial outlay of cash, leasing allows you to free up working capital for other profit-generating opportunities or investments.
- *Bank line of credit retention*—Business opportunities or unexpected demand for immediate cash should persuade you to retain bank lines of credit for more immediate access.
- *Tax benefits.* Dollar-for-dollar write-offs for the lease rental payments can make the depreciation of ownership far less attractive, thus allowing you to focus your profitable growth through the *use* of that asset, not necessarily *ownership* of it.
- *Danger of variable interest rates.* Unlike credit card companies and even some banks that offer business-equipment loans at an attractive promotional rate but with a dangerous variable interest rate thereafter, a true lease offers a consistent payment for the duration of the financing.
- *Obsolescence-proofing.* Leases provide an opportunity to add, upgrade, enhance, and even replace outdated or obsolete equipment. This flexibility allows you to minimize maintenance, repair, and operations (MRO) expenses that occur when you own that asset.
- *Budget consciousness.* Based on your capacity to allocate a consistent budget to finance equipment, most lease terms allow for purchase of the equipment, releasing of it, or the simple return to the lessor.
- *Credible sources.* From Siemens to Dell or Apple, many manufacturers, distributors, and resellers offer value-added leasing options.

So, what are the drawbacks to leasing? One is that you are likely to pay a higher price in the long run than for a straight purchase. And often, you have to retain the equipment for a prespecified period of time, which can be a challenge if your business fluctuates greatly.

When considering multiple leasing options, you should exercise due diligence to find out whether you are dealing with the leasing company directly or a broker, who often structures the deal and shops it around on your behalf. Although there is nothing of particular concern in dealing with legitimate brokers—they are similar to independent insurance agents, with intimate knowledge of the market—you may be able to eliminate the brokers' fees and commissions by dealing directly with the funding source.

FACTORING

Factoring is an interesting form of financing that actually helps to improve your cash flow without increasing your debt—and one that requires no change of control, entails no selling of equity in your business, and is fairly available regardless of your growth stage with the ability to scale. Factoring is the third-party purchase of your accounts receivable at a discount. Here is how it works: You sell a product or service to customers, who may not have the same sense of urgency in paying their invoices that your cash flow demands. For example, say your payroll is due on the 15th and 30th, but your clients pay you in 45-day cycles or even longer. To gain more immediate use of your money, you can sell the customer invoices (receivables) to a factor. However, before a factor buys that invoice, he or she will want to verify two critical attributes: first, that your customer has the means to pay that invoice, and second, that the customer actually received the product or service, has accepted it satisfactorily, and intends to pay. The factor then advances you a high percentage of the face value of the invoice and later collects the total amount of that invoice directly from your customer. When the customer pays the factor, the factor deducts his fee and refunds any remaining balance of the invoice to you. Fees range widely depending on the size of the invoice balance.

Some advantages to factoring include the following:

- *It is extremely quick.* Establish a relationship with a factor and funding can happen within two or three days. That immediate access to cash allows you to take on business that you may otherwise be forced to turn away in fear of not being able to meet cash-flow requirements.
- *It is often easier than applying for a loan.* Both the process and documentation are fairly straightforward in a factoring agreement.
- *It is available to most businesses.* You don't need a track record or good credit. What is critical is your customers' willingness and ability to pay their invoices.
- *It's not a loan.* You are not incurring debt. As your sales and revenue grow, there is no limit to how much you can factor.
- *Factors keep track of accounts receivable, aging, and collections.* This takes an administrative function off your plate.
- *Factors gauge customer satisfaction.* When they verify the viability of an invoice, one of their criteria is to ensure quality delivery.
- *Factors can speed up a customer's payment.* Most small companies seldom report their large customers to commercial credit agencies for delayed payments, but customers will often increase their payment frequency when a factor is involved, because they realize slow payment will be reported.

Here are some drawbacks to factoring:

- *It can be costly.* The cost can range from 5 to 25 percent of the invoice. Some kinds of invoices, such as construction, medical goods and services, and perishable goods, tend to be riskier because they require very specialized knowledge. The cost also heavily depends on customers and their creditworthiness and the volume and size of the invoices.
- *It has a perceived negative reputation.* Do you really want your customers to know you are struggling with cash flow? It could create an unnecessary fear that you are unable to produce and deliver your goods and services.
- *Your credibility is at risk by association.* How well do you really know the factoring company that will serve as an extension of you and your business?

- *No one factor will meet all of your business needs.* Some factors won't touch less than $100,000 a month in invoices, while others won't deal with more than $50,000. Many stay clear of labor-intensive industries such as contractors, construction, or medical services.
- *They are typically not interested in small and medium-size business customers.* Factors like to mitigate their risk by collecting invoices from large, reputable customers. They struggle and face increased administrative and collection expenses against a margin when attempting to collect invoices from smaller businesses.
- *Banks and factors don't compete.* There is less opportunity to negotiate the rate unless you compare factors with other factors. There is no FDIC insurance for your deposit. The credibility and viability of the factor could be a concern.

ROYALTIES AND LICENSING

Your company may be an ideal candidate for royalty or licensing financing if you happen to be:

- an established company with a hot product or service in demand,
- a growing company at the brink of launching a high-gross and high-net-margin product,
- a company that can easily raise prices without impacting sales, or
- a business that experiences an unusually aggressive correlation between its marketing efforts and sales results.

Royalty financing is a fairly new concept, offering an alternative to traditional debt financing. This type of capital is often an advance against future product or service revenues. The advance is paid back by remitting a percentage of those revenues back to the investor who provided the advance. It is often used to fund aggressive and capital-intensive sales and marketing campaigns in which the percentage of revenue can be easily paid from both the intense volume and high margins of the revenue generated. Capital amounts can range from as low as $50,000 up to millions of dollars, offered by a broad base of potential investors, including high-net-worth individuals and even local and state governments. This approach of selling a piece of the revenue stream instead of ownership can be structured over a fixed time frame or, as is often the case, until the investor has reached a certain return above the original principal.

What are some of the advantages to royalty financing?

- It doesn't require the entrepreneur to give up any equity or ownership in the company.
- The cost is directly related to the company's performance, often resulting in a win-win situation.
- There is no real need for an exit strategy—there is no cash out.

- It provides investors with a fairly liquid income-producing deal structure.
- If the investor has operating expertise, the royalty financing can also provide formal or informal mentoring.

Some potential drawbacks include these:

- The investor gets paid regardless of the profitability of the company or the sales and marketing campaign, and often gets paid first—before taxes, repayment of debt, and interest.
- Should the business fail, the investor continues to get paid even if the company declares Chapter 13 reorganization under the bankruptcy code. As long as there are sales, the investor gets paid.
- With equity contingencies, if the company is sold or goes public, investors may have warrants or options that would allow them to purchase shares in a company at often below-market rates.
- If your cost of goods sold fluctuates, it can easily erode high gross margins and the financial benefits of this revenue-sharing model.

Royalty financing is typically harder to find than more traditional financing and is often facilitated through introductions made by accountants and attorneys.

LICENSING

Another avenue to jump-start a new business, expand a current one, or perhaps improve the quality of your products and services in the current or perspective market position could be to license some or all of your existing intellectual property. This form of financing encompasses a licensing agreement as a partnership between that intellectual property owner (the licensor) and an interested party authorized to use that intellectual property (the licensee) in exchange for an agreed-upon payment (royalty or fee) over a period of time (term). The three most popular licensing strategies include:

- *Technology licensing agreements.* When a large software company integrates particular niche functionality from a smaller player, it is typically licensing that technology or intellectual property.
- *Trademark licensing or franchising agreements.* From quick-service restaurants to mobile veterinarians and even international hotel brands, a unique trademark or a repeatable and often predictable model for a unique concept can be franchised.
- *Copyright licensing agreements.* One example of a copyright licensing agreement is the publisher of a book licensing its copyrighted material to a producer of that book in digital formats such as e-books or audio CDs.

Many of these agreements are encompassed in a single contract, transferring the nature of the use of that intellectual property. Licensing agreements can also surface in the course of negotiating a joint venture, merger, or acquisition. Of particular interest in licensing, either as a licensor or licensee, are the expanded possibilities of new vertical markets, geographic territories, or additional customer profiles or ways to substantially enhance the benefits of an existing product or service. But beware: extensive legal descriptions are required for any licensing agreement in order to protect variations or reverse-engineering of the licensed intellectual property. Separately, in international markets, if that intellectual property is unprotected, you have no legal rights or recourse of its use by any other party.

INTERNATIONAL CAPITAL

With fluctuating exchange rates, many international investors seek to gain access to the U.S. market, one of the world's biggest economies, through foreign direct investment (FDI). Why not capture such investments in your own business?

Looking beyond the traditional U.S.-based financing options, international markets can provide interesting or unique approaches and product offerings and often considerably less expensive product development teams. Many entrepreneurs are finding great value in both the market and investors in hypergrowth markets such as China, India, and Eastern Europe.

Of particular interest to foreign investors—many of whom are conglomerates—is access to new or unique technologies with broad-based appeal to their existing businesses back home. Their global distribution can become a built-in channel for you overnight, not to mention a platform to launch other localized variations. Think of a digital application for U.S.-based mobile technology being expanded to work equally well, if not even better, on European or Asian wireless networks. Many foreign investors are less concerned about the short-term financial returns of their U.S. investments than they are about the strategic alliances and further market differentiation provided by the investment.

One extraordinary opportunity could be the Middle East—in particular, investment hotbeds such as Dubai. Not only do the wealthy Gulf States possess vast capital, but they also have a heightened interest in Western best practices, innovation, and accelerated time to market. These markets also provide an interesting gateway into Africa and Asia.

SPONSORSHIPS

If race cars, marathons, politicians, and Tiger Woods can all secure sponsors, why wouldn't you be able to do the same? If you think about what these examples have in common, it becomes a simple formula of enhanced or extended visibility and perceived value delivered to a target audience. Home Depot sponsors a NASCAR team, as many of the sport's fans also possess key customer attributes and an ideal do-it-yourself attitude. ING, the world's tenth largest financial institution, sponsors a myriad of high-profile marathon races, as the demographic of marathon runners is very consistent with that of a long-term, prudent investor. Accenture leverages Tiger's discipline, determination, and consistent execution to persuade its prospective clients to "Go on—be a tiger."

Exercise 6.1
Securing Corporate Sponsors

What are some of the best practices to enhance your opportunity to secure a corporate sponsor? Here is a checklist—see how your answers fit the bill.

1. Develop as complete a list as possible of the most relevant businesses for your campaign. Further dissect this list into quality tiers of primary, secondary, and tertiary candidates; primary organizations should be a natural fit, whereas tertiary candidates may be long shots but still worth the outreach effort.

---

2. Invest the time and effort for extensive due diligence about each organization's market presence, ideal customer and buyer profiles, and their existing channels to access that market.

---

3. Devise a quantifiable, unique attribute in one of the three critical points in question #2, above. For example: Help them expand their market reach, expand their customer or buyer base, accelerate their channel performance, or create new avenues to reach the same market at a reduced cost of sales.

---

4. Devise a succinct, professional executive summary of your proposed unique approach. Appeal to the corporate sponsors' logical self-interest, and in the process, make your products, services, and ideas an object of interest. Convince them to explore more.

---

5. Identify three to five trusted advisors to the most relevant executive responsible for corporate sponsorships and devise a strategy to create access to or an opportunity with that executive. (Read more about how to do this in my book *Relationship Economics* [Wiley, 2008].)

a. _____

b. _____

c. _____

d. _____

e. _____

If your company can demonstrate a direct correlation and unique added value between your products and services and the desired attributes of large corporate sponsors, this creative type of financing can provide a very high level of credible access and financial support in reaching a broad-based market.

Sponsorships are often planned well in advance and require contractual commitments. Often led by a sponsorship team within the marketing organization, they establish a specific set of criteria most relevant to the organization's strategic initiatives. Sponsors field hundreds, if not thousands, of inbound inquiries, filtering each submission based on the highest perceived return on investment (ROI). You are at a considerable advantage if you can put yourself in the sponsor's shoes and consider *why* they would want to be involved with you and your products or services and the specific benefits you can deliver. Equally critical, especially since it will make or break your success here, is to help them quantify their ROI.

A unique aspect of sponsorships that was uncovered in discussions with several creative entrepreneurs was their efforts to partner with a university foundation. This approach ensured compliance with Internal Revenue Service requirements for charitable contributions, and because the sponsorship was governed and administered by the foundation, the full amount of the sponsorship contribution was tax deductible by the corporate sponsors.

SUMMARY

☑ Alternative sources and access to creative capital, such as leasing, are often ignored.

☑ The flexibility, practicality, and cost-effectiveness of leasing can improve financial results through stabilizing cash flow and capital budgets.

☑ Factoring can help improve cash flow without increasing debt, requires no change of control or selling of equity in the business, and is fairly available regardless of the business's growth stage.

☑ Loyalty or licensing financing may be ideal for established companies with in-demand products or services that are on the brink of launching a high-gross and high-net-margin product with pricing flexibility.

☑ Technology, trademark, or copyright licensing can create access to new vertical markets, geographic territories, or additional customer segments or can substantially enhance the benefits of an existing product or service offering.

☑ With the fluctuating U.S. dollar, international capital in the form of FDI can create accelerated access to international markets, as well as less expensive product development with enhanced R&D resources.

☑ Enhanced or extended visibility and perceived value delivered to a target audience can open doors for sponsorship opportunities.

7

IPOs, Reverse Mergers, and International Markets

Sometimes savvy financial-engineering approaches to capital infusion include accessing the public market. Initial public offerings (IPOs), reverse mergers, and listing on foreign exchanges are often reserved for mature organizations that deem raising capital through the public market a viable option.

ACCESS TO THE PUBLIC MARKET

With the advent of Sarbanes-Oxley, compliance has become so stringent that turning to the public market is really one of the last resorts for most companies. As a matter of fact, in recent years, there has been a strong trend of publicly held companies going private via private equity financing. To take a public company private is not for the financial rookie CEO. Many CEOs are talked into these scenarios by service providers who may have the most to gain.

Other than investment markets with broad-based appeal, such as raising capital from angels, VCs, or PEGs mentioned earlier, the public market for capital is often a complicated, expensive one which requires a great deal more forethought. Whether you are considering it for the first time or have been through the process in the past, access to public capital requires a strong pool of knowledgeable assistance and the appropriate timeline to execute this complex process. A series of very intricate steps, particularly in the global capital market, can paint a public offering process in one market very differently from the same offering in a different market. The size of the offering, the particular industry, and the cost of both the process and ongoing compliance are all variables that entrepreneurs must consider if they are considering the public market today.

GOING PUBLIC

There were more public offerings on the NASDAQ exchange in 2007 than in any year since 2001. Although there was a significant reduction of early-stage ideas approaching the public market after the 2001 technology bubble, IPOs continued to climb every year through 2007.

Many experts recommend that if entrepreneurs are even contemplating taking their venture to the public market, they should begin to "act" like a public company as early as two years in advance of the desired IPO time frame. Steps such as preparation of detailed financial results on a consistent basis and a thorough business plan are critical (see figure 7.1).

The cast of characters to ensure smooth sailing through the process—dubbed the "IPO team"—will include the lead investment banking firm, an accounting firm, and a law firm. It is important to understand that these are not entry-level positions, and learning on the job will not suffice. You do not want to go into this process with rookies. They must possess direct,

Figure 7.1
The Typical IPO 12-Month Countdown Timeline

Once an IPO team (investment banker, legal counsel, SEC expert, outside auditor, public relations firm, etc.) has been formed, you can establish a plan and a basic timeline for the IPO Process.

Months before IPO	Activity
12	Recruit new management to run the public company—CEO, CFO, etc. Start compiling the financial information.
11	Start due-diligence work: write off worthless assets, resolve inconsistencies with Generally Accepted Accounting Principles (GAAP), and so forth.
10	Start drafting the prospectus. Coordinate the collection of data to minimize duplicative efforts.
9	Establish a board of directors for the newly formed public company.
8	Draft three-year historical financial statements.
7	Circulate the draft prospectus for comments.
6	Establish transition contracts for services and products that will now be provided to the newly formed public company. Some new contracts will be needed, such as independent audits of financial statements.
5	Finalize historical financial statements. Start preparing interim (stub) financial statements for the current period.
4	Finalize pro forma and interim financial statements. Make revisions to the draft prospectus.
3	Convene the new board of directors. Audit of interim financials should be complete.
2	Outside auditor's opinion is issued. Membership with stock exchange is complete.
1	File prospectus with Securities Exchange Commission (SEC). Issue a press release and sell the company to investors.

relevant, and extensive experience with IPOs that were deemed home runs. Also understand that this is a situation in which you get what you pay for. A frugal mentality here could create not only unnecessary expenses down the road but also, and more importantly, missed opportunities in the execution of the process—that is, in the total amount raised or the success of the IPO. You must recruit the most seasoned professionals your money can buy—this is no time for inexperienced MBAs fresh out of school.

Let's examine the five critical components or steps of the IPO process.

Step 1: Before You Officially Start

The IPO process typically begins eight weeks before the company officially registers with the Securities and Exchange Commission (SEC) with an all-hands meeting of the IPO team described above. At this meeting, all members of the team outline their critical roles and responsibilities as well as the timeline of the process. Because you are selling shares of your company to public investors, the investment banking firm becomes an "underwriter" of the stock sale to the public. Its extensive due-diligence investigation includes a deep dive into your company's financial performance, as well as that of its management team.

Other potential additions to the IPO team could include a public relations firm and a multitude of consultants primarily focused on operational efficiency and effectiveness, as well as profitable growth strategies in advance of, during, and after the process. Beyond the glitz and glamour, an enormous amount of hard work and work/life sacrifice is required by this core group of highly skilled professionals, who often work around the clock for a year or more.

Step 2: S-1 Registration and the Prospectus

The investment bank and the company work together to craft a preliminary prospectus and an S-1 registration statement to be filed with the SEC. The registration statement must contain the following six components:

- A detailed description of the company's business
- The names, addresses, salaries, and five-year business histories of each of the key officers
- The number of shares currently owned by each key officer (often referred to as a capitalization or cap table)
- The company's capitalization to date and a detailed description of the use to be made of proceeds from the public offering
- A list of any legal proceedings the company may be involved in, directly or indirectly
- A description of the company's target market, competitors, and growth strategies

Once the registration statement is filed with the SEC, the company enters a "quiet period" lasting until roughly thirty days after the stock begins to trade on the market. During this period, the company is prohibited from sending out any materials, other than the prospectus, in an effort not to influence public perception. Executives are forbidden from any public presentations or disclosures of the company's market position, performance, or future plans. For an example, see figure 7.2—the first page of Google's S-1 filing, dated April 29, 2004. (You'll also find the first ten pages in appendix B.) EDGAR Online, Inc. (NASDAQ: EDGR), is the public source to access any past prospectus or IPO filings.

Step 3: Early Interest

The investment bankers will discreetly engage the investor community for preferred interest and the possible range of the offering price. There is no commitment required by perspective buyers, since all official sales of the securities are prohibited until the SEC clears its registration. Once the registration statement has been cleared by both the SEC and relevant state security regulators, the investment bankers, along with the company, will finalize the prospectus and include the final price of the stock issued. It is critical to understand that the SEC's clearing of the registration statement does not constitute an approval or endorsement of any particular transaction. It simply affirms that the documentation has been reviewed for any errors or omissions. As a matter of fact, the SEC cannot even confirm the accuracy of the information in the filing—that is the job of the accounting auditors and law firm on the IPO team.

The time frame between filing the registration statement and the time the IPO starts trading is typically about eight to ten weeks.

Step 4: Getting on the Road

One of the most grueling steps in the IPO process is the whirlwind multi-city world tour, also referred to as the "road show." Although only a week or two in duration, the investment bank typically escorts the company's management to a new city every day to meet with prospective investors and review details of the business plan. The usual suspects include New York, San Francisco, Boston, Chicago, and Los Angeles, with appropriate international destinations such as London, Bahrain, Hong Kong, Sydney, and Tokyo.

A factor critical to the success of the IPO is the performance of the company's management team. If they are able to impress institutional investors, many will choose to purchase a considerable stake in the company. The typical or undersized entrepreneur is at a considerable disadvantage in the road-show process because only the largest institutional investors and sources of capital are invited to these private, highly exclusive gatherings. Average investors seldom hear the kind of detailed analysis and discussion of a company's business in the prospectus as they do in verbal discussions at these

Figure 7.2
The First Page of Google's S-1 Filing

As filed with the Securities and Exchange Commission on *April 29, 2004*
Registration No. 333-

SECURITIES AND EXCHANGE COMMISSION
Washington, D.C. 20549

FORM S-1
REGISTRATION STATEMENT
Under
The Securities Act of 1933

GOOGLE INC.
(Exact name of Registrant as specified in its charter)

Delaware	7375	77-0493581
(State or other jurisdiction of incorporation or organization)	(Primary Standard Industrial Classification Code Number)	(I.R.S. Employer Identification Number)

1600 Amphitheatre Parkway
Mountain View, CA 94043
(650) 623-4000
(Address, including zip code, and telephone number, including area code, of Registrant's principal executive offices)

Eric Schmidt
Chief Executive Officer
Google Inc.
1600 Amphitheatre Parkway
Mountain View, CA 94043
(650) 623-4000
(Name, address, including zip code, and telephone number, including area code, of agent for service)

Copies to:

Larry W. Sonsini, Esq.	David C. Drummond, Esq.	William H. Hinman, Jr., Esq.
David J. Segre, Esq.	Jeffery L. Donovan, Esq.	Simpson Thacher & Bartlett
Wilson Sonsini Goodrich & Rosati,	Anna Itoi, Esq.	LLP
P.C.	Google Inc.	3330 Hillview Avenue
650 Page Mill Road	1600 Amphitheatre	Palo Alto, California 94304
Palo Alto, California 94304-1050	Parkway	(650) 251-5000
(650) 493-9300	Mountain View, CA 94043	
	(650) 623-4000	

Approximate date of commencement of proposed sale to the public: As soon as practicable after the effective date of this Registration Statement.

If any of the securities being registered on this Form are being offered on a delayed or continuous basis pursuant to Rule 415 under the Securities Act of 1933, as amended (the *"Securities Act"*), check the following box.

If this Form is filed to register additional securities for an offering pursuant to Rule 462(b) under the Securities Act, please check the following box and list the Securities Act registration number of the earlier effective registration statement for the same offering.

If this Form is a post-effective amendment filed pursuant to Rule 462(c) under the Securities Act, check the following box and list the Securities Act registration number of the earlier effective registration statement for the same offering.

private gatherings. (Because smaller companies cannot afford to engage high-profile investment bankers, they are seldom invited to these plush events and therefore lack the access to large institutional investors. Along the same lines, the average investor does not get invited to these events, so they often don't get a clear picture of what the company is really up to.)

The road show heavily influences the final price and size of the offering. The expected demand for the deal, along with other relevant market conditions, creates a unique balancing act between the company's need to raise as much capital as possible and the investors' need to see their stock purchase generate a fairly quick appreciation.

The offering price and size can result in three scenarios:

- A hot or in-demand offering can create a premium price and enhance the size of the offering right out of the gate (think of Google, Apple, and the like).
- Lukewarm interest in the road show could actually decrease the size of the offering, leading to a reduction in the initial per-share price.
- Insufficient demand or a cold shoulder at the road show have caused IPOs to be postponed.

Step 5: Let the Trading Begin

The investment bank typically puts together a syndicate of other investment bankers in a viral effort to distribute the IPO—because many IPOs may be too expansive to be covered by a single bank—and they offer this IPO to their preferred clients, in essence taking their best deals to clients with whom they can maximize both their commission and trading volumes.

The investment bank—beyond the preparation fee—profits from the spread between the stock acquisition cost by the issuing company and the price that it is offered to the public (for example, the investment bank buys the stock from you at $10 per share and sells to the public at $12 per share, keeping the $2 spread).

Once the offering price (the initial trading price of the stock) has been set and potential investors receive the final prospectus, an IPO is declared effective. This typically occurs after the market closes on the night before the stock begins to trade, while the lead investment banker confirms a series of buy orders. That lead investment banker is also responsible for the smooth flow of transactions in the first few days of the trading. In an effort to stabilize the stock price, the investment bank is legally allowed to buy its own block of shares. It can also impose a penalty to brokers to discourage short-term flipping of that stock.

An IPO is declared final typically seven days after the company's debut. In very rare instances, an IPO can be canceled after the stock begins to trade, in which case all of the transactions are null and void and any financial commitments are returned.

In what is also referred to as the "lock-up period," company insiders and directors are usually restricted for six months (180 days) from selling their own shares after the initial IPO trading.

As you consider an IPO, keep in mind that there are some significant disadvantages:

- Once you accept public capital, you enter a very different and transparent "public life" where every aspect of the company and, in particular, its management, performance, behaviors, and even unintentional signals will be scrutinized by a horde of analysts, the press, and individual shareholders.
- Servicing investors, the SEC, and countless other interested parties is an expensive time- and resource-intensive proposition. From analyst calls to shareholder meetings, the investment of time in preparation, interaction, and follow-through is dramatically increased.
- There are exponential costs associated with the more complex accounting and director liability insurance fees.
- For many public company CEOs, the demands of consistent quarterly performance often dictate short-term behaviors instead of a long-term view of the market opportunities.

The public market is the single biggest source of capital, and it should not be overlooked. Yet for many companies, the IPO process is a grueling test of patience, discipline, and consistent execution. The success of the IPO is directly correlated with the advanced planning and caliber of the IPO team you are willing and able to recruit.

REVERSE MERGERS

Another access to the public market is through the back door—often referred to as a reverse merger. This is a simplified fast-track method in which a private company acquires shares of a publicly traded but inactive company.

If you don't need capital quickly, yet anticipate substantial growth in size and scale that will let you prosper as a public entity—typically $20 million in revenues and $2 million in earnings—there are thousands of these inactive public companies, often referred to as "shells." The opportunity to appeal to the broader public investment community through a shell is attractive. Public funding is much more abundant, and the market can provide a greater supply of equity capital for public companies than private funding options can.

Capital infusions from reverse mergers have been used for a broad array of purposes such as product development and working capital, as well as for a roll-up—a consolidation of a number of small yet complementary or synergistic private companies into one larger entity. In 1996, one study estimated that 53 percent of all companies obtaining a public stock listing did so through reverse mergers. That figure dropped to roughly 30 percent by 2000 and was considerably less during the tech bubble as countless investment bankers gained a huge appetite for what seemed to be daily IPOs.

Reverse mergers can be a bit deceiving due to the fact that the initial transaction of acquiring the shell gets you only halfway there. Once public, you still need to raise capital. Though not as high as a traditional IPO, the expense of a reverse merger is also considerable. Deals in the $75,000 to $500,000 range often cost 15 to 50 percent of traditional IPO expenses in fees. Beyond the initial transaction cost, the acquiring company may also have to give up 10 to 20 percent of its ownership, in essence paying for the privilege of going public. As the company generates more capital, it will also have to give up additional equity and control.

Although finding a shell and going through the initial transaction are considerably easier than a traditional IPO, the real challenge becomes the critical need to create public market buzz and as such a real interest in trading volume for the stock.

If a reverse merger is a viable alternative to a traditional IPO for your business, here are the three key steps:

1. *Identify a shell company.* There are a slew of merchant bankers, brokers, and consultants who specialize in this process. Law firms with securities practices have even been known to have an inactive company sitting on a partner's desk. Accountants also tend to keep financial records of inactive client companies. The ideal scenario is a made-to-order shell without possible headaches from a business failure of that company. Beware that in many transactions, a challenging cost of reverse-merger transactions is having to relinquish equity—typically between 2 and 5 percent—to principals of the shell company and potentially also to financial advisors who aid in the process.
2. *Devise an "after the transaction" financing strategy.* The initial transaction to acquire the shell and become publicly listed is only half the battle. It is critical that the entrepreneur have a strategy for raising successful capital after getting on the public market. Two common approaches are registering the common stock shares with the SEC or issuing warrants through a brokerage firm. I cannot emphasize enough how carefully deals must be structured—specifically the number of shares owned by investors and the establishment of a new quote after inactive shares have been cleaned up.
3. *Move beyond the stigma.* Because reverse mergers are not easily understood or broadly practiced, they tend to have a bad reputation. André Schnabl from the respected accounting firm Grant Thornton LLP describes that although many reputable entities have executed successful reverse mergers, that in general reverse mergers can have hidden risks, requiring more financial due diligence than one might otherwise expect. André believes that reverse mergers have received a bad reputation because they may represent an easier and cheaper way to the capital market. Unknown risks may be lurking around the corner and extensive due diligence is often overlooked.
   Describing how Grant Thornton LLP mitigates these issues, André says, "We as an organization are very careful of the promoters and

evaluating the intention behind the transaction." Often, the credibility and reputation of the firm and key individuals involved with a legitimate reverse merger far outweigh the unknown backgrounds or history of those who express an interest in this area.

Exercise 7.1
Your Reverse Merger

If you believe a reverse merger would be a good idea for your company, consider each step in the process and answer the following questions.
1. Where would you begin your search for a possible shell company?

_____

_____

2. Who do you know that is knowledgeable about raising capital successfully with a reverse merger? Where would you start surrounding yourself with an "A-team"?

_____

_____

3. What questions are you forgetting to ask?

_____

_____

_____

Despite the risks, there have been some high-profile and successful reverse mergers. In the 1950s, for example, Armand Hammer, the world-renowned oil magnate and industrialist, invested in the Shell company, in which he merged one of his strongest winners, Occidental Petroleum. In 1970, Ted Turner completed a reverse merger with Rice Broadcasting, which went on to become Turner Broadcasting. In 1996, Muriel Siebert, the first woman member of the New York Stock Exchange, took her investment brokerage firm public through a reverse merger with J. Michael & Sons, a defunct Brooklyn furniture company. One of the dot-com fallen angels, Rare Medium, merged with a less-than-exciting refrigeration company and transformed the business. In the process, it turned a $2 stock in 1998 to one worth more than $90 per share just two years later.

Because barriers to entry in this field are low, scams and unscrupulous behavior are more common than one might imagine. By garnering large stakes in the free trading shares of the shell company, scam artists combine a marginal private company and a massive publicity campaign with the sole intent of attracting unsuspecting individual investors. Unrealistic promises and outlandish performance claims create hyped trading volumes that allow the scam artists to sell their shares. This "pump and dump" process eventually leads to unsuspecting investors losing all of their money, and then some.

LISTING ON FOREIGN EXCHANGES

Similar to the way you can promote your products and services abroad, U.S. companies of all sizes can also participate in listings on various international exchanges. At the end of 1990, there were an estimated 2,000 foreign listings on the twelve European Union countries' stock exchanges. In 2007, China led the world in the number of IPOs (209) and capital raised ($52.6 billion). The United States ranked second in capital raised ($38.7 billion) and third for IPOs (178), after Australia (189). Brazil ranked third in capital raised ($29 billion).

Emerging markets in 2008 continued to drive global IPOs, accounting for fourteen out of the twenty largest. According to the Ernst & Young publication *Globalization: Global IPO Trends Report 2007* (2007), fifty-one exchanges exist worldwide, with a total market capitalization of $50.6 trillion. The top six exchanges are:

* New York Stock Exchange (NYSE)
* NASDAQ
* Tokyo Stock Exchange
* London Stock Exchange
* Euronext (in April 2007, Paris-based Euronext merged with the NYSE, combining exchanges in Paris, London, Brussels, Amsterdam, and Lisbon with New York)
* Hong Kong Stock Exchange (HKSE)

North America is no longer the major player, representing only one-third of the global capital market. The U.S. economy is also shrinking as a percentage of the gross world product. China, along with the other emerging markets in the BRIC countries (Brazil, Russia, India, and China), has considerably higher growth rates than most developed countries. These high-growth-rate economies present the opportunity for potentially higher returns for global investors. In China, second-tier financial institutions and insurance companies are privatizing and going public. (The largest Chinese IPO happened in 2006 when the state-owned Industrial and Commercial Bank of China went public, raising $22 billion on the HKSE, allowing for foreign investors.)

The globalization of stock exchange markets has increased competition for desired listings, as well as providing an exponential increase in both private and institutional investors. No longer are the NYSE and NASDAQ your only viable options; access to foreign capital—via foreign investors—at a time where the U.S. dollar is at its weakest valuations, may also be a viable alternative. Depending on your company's long-term business and financial objectives, raising capital from foreign markets can help.

One challenge of raising capital from foreign markets is the manner in which financial statements are prepared. Companies must adhere to a complex set of rules that are similar to those that the SEC requires of foreign entities interested in being listed as a U.S. security. The International

Organization of Securities Commissions (IOSCO) is attempting to create a global set of standards consistent with the U.S. GAAP (Generally Accepted Accounting Principles). Regulators must balance the need to protect with the desire to attract the rest of the world.

So, where do you begin? As is the case when you evaluate any and all financing options, it is critical to have a thorough plan in place before you start. A number of consulting firms specialize in international business, and an increasing number of expatriates are returning home to attract U.S.-based companies abroad.

A great starting point may be to visit the country you aim to target for a business venture. Establishing contacts and experiencing local business acumen will help ensure that any investments from that country or region are prudent. A long-term commitment to the success of an international venture takes a lot of time and money without an immediate return on your investment. Cultural, political, and economic profiles for the country provide local information about valuable regional zoning laws and insights into the stability of the political climate. A stable currency and understanding the cost of local sourcing, customs regulations, and the unique nuances in the workings of foreign banks are crucial.

Joint ventures with companies in your target country, while employing local accounting, legal, and consulting resources familiar with both inbound and outbound ventures, will help mitigate countless risks in the process. Understanding the cultural differences and accepting that the rest of the world simply does not do business like we do here in the United States are essential to avoiding frustration. For example, the pace is considerably slower in Italy, Greece, Malaysia, and Brazil—it is much more difficult to quickly verify financial information there than in the United States.

Choose partners who are good conversationalists and fluent in U.S. business practices. A specific focus on an international market with intimate knowledge of the language and culture consistently remains a unique differentiator in those you choose to engage in supporting your efforts to raise capital internationally.

Here is a ten-point checklist to consider when deciding if raising capital abroad is worth exploring for your business:

1. *International appeal.* Will your products or services be of particular interest or value to international customers? Is there international demand for their benefits with the ability to generate profitable returns? Make certain you are less mesmerized by the glamour of raising international capital and more grounded by its application.
2. *In it for the long haul.* As mentioned earlier, any inclinations to raise capital abroad requires long-term perspective of longevity and success in those international markets versus short-term transactions. Although it is fairly easy to begin investigations in international markets, succeeding with international sources of capital will require a commitment to follow up, follow through, and make several return trips to nurture the necessary critical relationships.

3. *International channels.* It will always be less expensive for a local distributor to take your products and services and sell them down the street than it will be for you to fly or ship containers across oceans for the same sale. Access to foreign markets will require prudent due diligence and establishment of existing channel infrastructures with local relationships on the ground in your target international markets.

4. *Export cents.* Will it cost you more to engage in the export process documentation and expense than to look for that same capital in your own backyard?

5. *Import regulations.* What are the U.S. import rules and regulations you must adhere to if that foreign investor demands inbound access to U.S. markets through an investment in your company?

6. *Information transfer.* The transfer of intellectual property, often through licensing as discussed in chapter 6, can add an extra layer of complexity if that intellectual property is not protected in the local market. Employing knowledgeable local intellectual property attorneys will be critical.

7. *International payments.* How will you accept letters of credit from overseas buyers and coordinate international payments with your local bank, suppliers, and legal council? What happens when the currency fluctuates?

8. *Insurance abroad.* In the process of transporting your goods and delivering your services, how will you protect your assets? Both government and quasi-governmental entities such as the U.S. Import-Export Bank (see Appendix A for more details) offer private insurance to cover the commercial and political risks associated with foreign investments.

9. *Global logistics.* How do you plan to keep ice cream cold in Dubai when the average August temperatures can reach upwards of 120 degrees Fahrenheit? The transport, logistics, and asset management in getting goods and services carefully packaged and diligently transported is the key to success.

10. *Global debt.* How will you collect global account receivables? What knowledge do you have or can you obtain regarding foreign courts should an investment deal go bad? The appropriate contract clauses governing arbitration or dispute resolution to reduce risk and ensure against bad debt will help retain operating margins against that investment capital you have raised.

Raising capital abroad is time consuming and complicated. It's best to begin, as noted here, by doing business abroad. Once you start that, the avenues to raising capital in other countries will begin to appear.

SUMMARY

☑ Mature organizations or hypergrowth firms can leverage financial-engineering approaches through IPOs, listings on foreign exchanges, and reverse mergers.

☑   With the advent of more stringent governance and compliance requirements, such as Sarbanes-Oxley, turning to the public market is one of the
last resorts for many companies.

☑   Other than markets with broad-based appeal, the public market is often a
complicated, expensive place, and one that will require a great deal of forethought, a strong pool of knowledgeable helpers, and the appropriate timeline to execute this complex process.

☑   The IPO process is comprised of five critical steps, from assembling the IPO
team and registering with the SEC, to creating preliminary interest, conducting a road show, and finally, actually trading.

☑   A simplified fast-track method in which a private company acquires shares
of an inactive publicly traded one—referred to as a reverse merger—is
another path to the public market.

☑   Although 15 to 50 percent less expensive than traditional IPOs, reverse
mergers can be a bit deceiving as, after the initial transaction of acquiring
the shell, you will still need to raise capital.

☑   U.S. companies of all sizes can also participate in listings on various international exchanges in London, Tokyo, Hong Kong, and elsewhere.

☑   The international appeal of a company's products and services, along with a
host of international financing, accounting, legal, and logistics obstacles,
must be strongly considered.

8

Valuations, Acquisitions, and Exit Strategies

If you're thinking about giving employees equity in your business, merging your business with another company, raising outside capital, or selling out—in essence, doing any deal that may alter the ownership of your business—a fundamental question will be, "How much is it worth?" Valuation is simply a tool to help answer what both your hard assets (like inventory and equipment) and your soft assets (intellectual property, brand name, and so on) are worth.

The essence of an acquisition—whether you are acquiring a business or another business is acquiring yours—has a lot to do with your current and anticipated market position. Ideally, the two companies combined will be worth more than each standing alone.

An "exit strategy" is simply a fancy way of charting how you will one day separate yourself from your business—hopefully with a pocketful of cash. Let's take a closer look at all three topics.

WORTH OF A COMPANY

How do you know what your company is worth? There is a whole industry that uses both art and science to determine the current value of a company, as well as the current or future value of any single initiative, project, or financing event.

This is a critical step and one that comes into play not only in more effectively engaging employees but also in raising capital from investors, selling an asset, or retiring a partner. If you undervalue your business, you will give away more than you should. Overvalue it, and you'll turn off investors.

To do it right, both art and science are needed. The *science* is financial engineering, used to evaluate cash flow, revenue growth, and the value of assets over some period of time. It incorporates standard deviations, averages, and a multitude of other mathematical variables. The *art* comes from the experience of knowing the right scenario in which to apply the appropriate valuation, approach, or model. In hindsight, the dangerous flaw during the dot-com era was that battle-tested, proven valuation models gave way to euphoria, hype, and often unsubstantiated attributes such as "eyeballs" (how many individuals saw a Web site), "click-thrus" (when a visitor accesses one site through another), and customer acquisition costs.

Valuations

Tim Koller, Marc Goedhart, and David Wessels from McKinsey & Co., in their book *Valuation: Measuring and Managing the Value of Companies* (4th ed., 2005), have captured an extensive body of knowledge, ranging from the company value to the practitioner's approach to cash-flow valuation, to the application of various valuation models. According to the authors, valuation—the process of determining the current value of an asset or a company—is particularly useful in the following four scenarios:

1. Estimating the value of alternative business strategies, including key strategic initiatives such as new product development, capital expenditure, joint ventures, or new market entries
2. Assessing major transactions such as raising capital, mergers, acquisitions, divestitures, recapitalization, and share repurchases
3. Conducting a value-based management review to analyze the quantifiable performance of a business operation
4. Communicating with key stakeholders regarding fluctuation in the value of the business

The fundamental premise in the valuation of a company is its ability to generate cash flow and a consistent return on investments. Managing current or future shareholder value expectations is critical in retaining the long-term support of the shareholders.

Developing value-creation-based performance metrics for your entire company will help pave the way for much smoother growth, as well as for the ability to manage value effectively. Only by focusing on cash flow and cash-flow rates of return from various business investments can you quantify the value you've created in the business.

For most entrepreneurs, two general approaches to valuation are appropriate:

1. Discounted Cash Flow (DCF) valuation
2. Relative valuation

Let's examine each approach and under what circumstances it would be most applicable.

Discounted Cash Flow Valuation

Let's start with a simple definition: *Discounted cash flow* is a valuation for an investment arrived at by estimating future cash flows while at the same time considering a measure of risk. Think of it as a required rate of return on that investment over a particular period of time. The DCF is calculated using various formulas—you can easily find different version, with explanations, on the Web. Unless you have a good head for numbers, however, it is probably a wise move to engage an expert to help you perform a DCF analysis.

Like any other tool, what you input to the formula will dramatically affect the accuracy of the output. As such, key questions in determining valuation via DCF are:

- Which cash flows will you discount?
- What is the anticipated growth rate for the business or investment?
- What is the appropriate discount (imputed interest) rate?
- Over what period of time do you expect cash to flow?

Again, seek the help of a competent accountant or financier to arrive at a valuation using DCF.

Relative Valuation

Relative valuation is a lot like the "comparable" information you get from your real estate agent or mortgage lender about the other homes for sale in your neighborhood—independent assessments by the market for a similar or comparable asset (in this case, your company rather than your home). As such, to do relative valuations effectively, you need to identify comparable assets (perhaps your competitors or similar firms you've worked with in the past) and obtain independent market values for these assets. Merchant or investment bankers are always a good source for this information. It is critical to consider any factors that may affect the applicability of this information, such as differences in the market size they serve, the geography they operate in, or their repeat-versus-new business percentages.

Relative value, when used consistently, is commonly referred to in terms of "multiples." Investment bankers often talk about having helped a client buy or sell a company at "*X* multiple of earnings." Multiples are derived from common variables such as earnings, cash flow, book value, or revenues. There are four steps to understanding multiples:

1. *Define the multiple.* It is critical that the multiple be defined consistently. Specifically, the value of the equity should be divided by equity earnings or its book value. For example, a multiple based on earnings should be applied consistently across different assets.
2. *Describe the multiple.* The average, standard deviation, median, and outliers will help avoid scenarios where multiples cannot be estimated or where they may lead to biased estimates. Typically, two or three different independent sources may create a multiple of a company; you simply take the average of the three findings. Alternatively, you can throw out the high and the low and accept the middle one.

3. *Analyze the multiple.* What are the fundamentals that determine and drive these multiples, such as growth, risk, and cash-flow patterns? More importantly, how do the changes in these fundamentals change the multiple? For example, if company A has twice the growth rate of company B, it will generally not trade at twice the multiple.

4. *Apply the multiple.* How do you define a "comparable" company? Even within the same sectors, traditionally perceived comparable firms with very different fundamentals will yield different multiples. There is no reason why a firm cannot be compared to another firm in a very different business if the two firms have the same risk, growth, and cash-flow characteristics. It is often impossible to find a firm exactly identical to the one you are valuing.

Whether you are working with an expert or doing it yourself, according to valuation expert Michael Pellegrino of www.valuationinfo.com, six factors come into considerable play when assessing the value of an asset:

1. *Value proposition:* What benefit do your customers get from your products or services?
2. *Market analysis:* Is your business on the leading edge of a market or getting a growing share of a shrinking market?
3. *Financials:* What has been your past financial performance and forecast for the future?
4. *Previous capital raises:* What independent third party was willing to pay for a piece of your business and how much did they pay?
5. *Competition:* Similar to appraisals of comparable homes, what are the competing products or services that may affect your revenues?
6. *Regulatory hurdles:* What regulatory processes are involved in getting your product or service to market? The more there are, the more likely they will have effects on its value.

ACQUISITIONS

Sometimes, another avenue to growing your business may not involve raising outside capital. Beyond their organic growth, many companies look to grow inorganically by acquiring competitors or other companies that would enhance their market position or product portfolio or simply provide them additional customers at a significantly reduced cost of acquiring those customers. I've also seen raising capital become considerably easier (though it's never easy) when there is an opportunity for the investors to roll up a group of smaller operators into a stronger, more diversified whole.

According to a recent PricewaterhouseCoopers (PwC) survey of fast-growing private companies with annual revenues ranging from $5 million to $150 million, more than half of the CEOs said that joint ventures, strategic alliances, and acquisitions are critical to growing a business and moving into new markets. However, almost half of the 339 respondents also said that they were not looking to engage in any acquisition or merger activity in the foreseeable future, citing concerns over costs, lack of attractive business targets, and unsuccessful postmerger integration.

While strategic alliances or perhaps even mergers and acquisitions (M&A) may be an attractive growth strategy for certain businesses, smaller companies face increasing complexities and costs of integration, in addition to managing their day-to-day business. Smaller company acquisitions are often as complex as those of larger corporations. The challenge for many entrepreneurs is that they typically don't have the in-house expertise or resources to engage external subject matter experts (similar to the IPO team discussed in the previous chapter, including investment bankers, lawyers, accountants, and public relations experts) to support, and even own, the process.

The sheer failure rate of many such partnerships, however, mandates that entrepreneurs must be willing and able to invest the required time and money into successful alliances and acquisitions. Studies quoted in David Harding and Sam Rovit's book *Mastering the Merger: Four Critical Decisions That Make or Break the Deal* (2004) show that 60 to 70 percent of all acquisitions fail, and that nearly 90 percent of all acquired businesses lose market share. Consequently, in many cases, the buyers are worse off than before the transaction. Few growth strategies built on acquisition are compelling or likely to produce superior results. Although there are some great examples, in general, acquisitions are difficult to complete and fraught with surprises.

The human resources questions of any merger or acquisition process are often some of the most difficult to ask and even more difficult to answer. What does the management team of the target company want—to retire or to come along for the ride? Do you have enough management expertise to accommodate them? Will your management team be able to become "employees" and work for someone else?

Geographic considerations require another critical thought process. Do you want to make acquisitions to expand into other areas? It might make sense to have a footprint in those additional regions.

Maybe you want to expand your product line. Maybe you want to enter a new market with a new type of customer. If you join with a company doing $10 million in sales, another doing $40 million, and another doing $20 million, you can become a $100 million company. As the business increases in scale, you can negotiate better deals with your vendors and suppliers and eliminate duplicate positions, and so forth.

Identifying and integrating successful alliance partnerships requires a solid understanding of valuations, extensive due diligence, and a clear grasp on whether or not the target partner company is a good strategic fit with your overall (and hopefully profitable) growth plans. Identifying and structuring the deal is half the battle. Plan to invest significant time, effort, and companywide (internal and external) resources to integrate after the acquisition, because this will often make or break the original synergies that you perceived to be of quantifiable value in embarking on this journey.

So, when is an acquisition opportunity right for your business? Why add the additional headache and frustrations to your existing day-to-day challenges? Do you really need someone else's challenges to compound yours?

In the PwC survey mentioned earlier:

- Sixty-three percent of the companies said that extending their customer base was the main reason they considered a merger or acquisition of a new business.
- Thirty-seven percent said that they used a merger or acquisition to expand into new markets.
- Twenty-eight percent cited reduction of shared costs of geographic expansion—often into domestic or international regions where there was no previous presence.
- Sixteen percent mentioned an expansion of their product or service portfolio and an alternative to existing research and development efforts.

Here are a few other interesting facts:

- Close to 50 percent said they had participated in five strategic alliance relationships over the previous three years.
- Twenty-seven percent had merged with or acquired two companies.
- Twenty-five percent were involved in licensing or comarketing arrangements with other companies.

A Successful Acquisition Strategy

Here are five critical elements to a successful acquisition strategy:

1. *The "why" and the "how" are as critical as the "what."* Sit down (ideally in a quiet place, away from the minutiae of the day) and really think through one big question: *Why do you want to do this?* Is it to add to your current customer portfolio, to reduce the cost of acquiring those customers, to increase your product or service offerings, or to add critical employees to "own" important operating parts of the business? What quantifiable outcomes will you achieve as a result of this acquisition?
2. Answers to these and other critical "goals and objectives" questions will address which specific companies you should target for acquisition, what price ranges you're willing to pay for each, and the manner in which you integrate them into your core business. Ignore this step and you'll waste countless hours looking at deals that are incongruent with your core strength. You will make acquisition decisions based on emotional preferences and fail to integrate the real value that you may see before you start the process.

    Put more than one egg in that basket. It is inherently dangerous to put all of your eggs in one basket! In other words, don't bet the business on any single acquisition. There is a rule of thumb when it comes to small company acquisitions: out of three, one will be a home run, one will be mediocre, and one will outright fail. Make sure you're not taking on more risk than you can live with if your next acquisition is the one that doesn't work.

3. *Buy fewer, but buy for quality.* My mother drove into me this philosophy: buy fewer clothes, she said, but buy better-quality brands than you think you can afford. Not only will you look better in them, but they will last much longer and cost you less to maintain and replace. Acquisitions work the same way. I've met entrepreneurs, investors, and board members who equate acquisitions to some kind of game like "capture the flag." They view growth through acquisitions as a badge of honor and as fodder for stories they can tell to their golf or poker buddies at the country club.

   The astute entrepreneur realizes that fewer, *quality* acquisitions will trump any larger number of random acquisitions—especially if you don't have the experience in turnarounds of problem companies, employees, customers, distribution channels, and, worst of all, bitter shareholders. Problem companies always cost twice as much and take twice as long to fix than you can possibly imagine or anticipate.

4. *This is not the right time or place to skimp.* I'm a huge supporter of entrepreneurs who are frugal and believe that every single dollar matters when it comes to how they invest and where they save. But M&A is not a place to skimp on critical resources in the preparation (due diligence), interaction (getting the deal done), and follow-through (postacquisition integration) stages of this critical process.

   It's imperative that you staff your campaign with experienced professionals—those who do transactions for a living (externally, this could be an investment banker who focuses on your size of company, industry, or acquisition target companies; internally, it's a corporate development officer responsible for this operating function of your business) and hold them accountable for executing your strategy.

   You also need to fund their efforts with the appropriate budget. Allocating minimal resources for research will deliver inadequate due diligence. Insufficient resources for assessment of the incoming team will often lead to good people in really bad positions. Lack of resources for marketing and business development of the new products or services added to the mix will fail to deliver the additional customers you expect.

5. *It won't be a "bargain" if it fails.* How much are you willing to pay for an acquisition and what price are they willing to accept to join your business? Whether you're setting your price, offering one, or contemplating accepting one—this is where most entrepreneurs screw up the deal before they even start.

   Ask for an unrealistic valuation of your business, and most investors or acquisition suitors will walk. Offer too low a multiple, and likewise the company you're trying to partner with and integrate into the future of your business will pass you by. Overpay for an asset, and you could easily pressure the other valves in the revenue-and-profit-generation engine of the business. This is where a sharp investment banker with a thorough analysis of market conditions and of this specific acquisition opportunity can really help.

   Unfortunately, I've seen some tight-fisted entrepreneurs who have found an undervalued asset and then negotiated a good deal into a bad one. In the process of squeezing every ounce of blood they can from that stone, they create resentment in the incoming people—all the way down to the bone of critical infrastructure resources. They then spend countless days, weeks, and months trying to fix something they could have avoided in the process. Keep in mind that an acquisition will never be a bargain if it fails. As a matter of fact, "bargain-basement deals" tend to cost you more in the long run than they'll ever be worth!

Putting the Acquisitions Strategy to Use

Throughout his career, Rusty Gordon, the former CEO of Knowlagent, has done a number of acquisitions, and he has more belief in them than most other CEOs I interviewed. He reiterates, however, that they are very difficult to do successfully, citing the quality of the management team and their experiences in having both initiated the process as acquirers and lived on the other side of the table as takeover targets.

"There are many products masquerading as companies out there," Rusty says. "Acquisitions can sometimes be beneficial when you have a strong single product offering and the acquisition of another product will give you access to a larger piece of business from the customer."

In terms of financing an acquisition, most banks will work with an entrepreneur to put together a line of credit specifically for that purpose. They then establish a set of benchmarks that each acquisition has to meet in order to qualify for funding under that program. For example, the acquisition has to produce a certain amount of EBITDA (earnings before interest, taxes, depreciation, and amortization), positive cash flow, and so on, within a certain time frame.

In the PwC survey referenced earlier, 49 percent of CEOs polled said they would not look to acquire or merge with another company because they were pleased with their current organic growth strategy. Nearly 30 percent expressed fear of "biting off more than they can chew," while 24 percent mentioned a consistent lack of interesting companies to acquire.

Entrepreneurs can certainly increase their probability of success by enlisting the advice of board members, investors, and other internal and external advisors experienced in acquisition strategies. Many of these experts can help you structure and capitalize your company properly so that it can withstand any strain from acquisitions. They can also assist you in refining your strategy, identifying target companies, negotiating with management, and performing due diligence on the good, the bad, and the ugly aspects of the deal. They can help you achieve your goal of growth through acquisition while allowing your core business to continue to flourish.

Many experts firmly believe that acquisitions should be a part of your overall business strategy. Just remember that, more often than not, they fail or are ultimately deemed unsuccessful. As a nimble, small business, you also have the option of looking at alliances, joint ventures, and licensing as ways to grow your business as viable alternatives to full-blown acquisitions. All of these options also help predetermine or support your exit strategy.

EXIT STRATEGIES

Most entrepreneurs begin their companies with a game plan—a strategy of where to compete (your market), how to compete (your products and services), and your unique differentiation (that which will drive your performance metrics). Yet, even though most understand that, at some point, the end of their stewardship of the business will come (by choice or by force of nature—which includes investors), many entrepreneurs remain ill-prepared in their efforts to develop and update an exit strategy. Think of this as your living will and last testament for the business. Your investors will inevitably demand it—and some may force you to act upon it sooner than you'd prefer.

Although you may not think you need an exit strategy now, a number of surprise events—including natural causes—could force you to move on earlier than you originally planned. For example, I fly extensively for speaking, training, and consulting engagements, and there isn't a trip where I don't think about what would happen if (God forbid) I didn't make it. What if, during a routine trip to a client meeting, I was involved in a car accident and became disabled to the point that I could no longer meet the demands of running our small business?

Do you have investors, business partners, or your spouse as shareholders in the company? What would happen to the company if you decided to part ways with your business partners or to get divorced? These unexpected events, and a whole slew of others, make a documented exit strategy critical for every entrepreneur.

Investors in general, and institutional investors in particular, do not have time to "dabble." They are typically not your relatives and, although most entrepreneurs begin their relationships with outside investors from a point of trust and credibility, if either is diluted, you're likely to be asked to step aside.

Investors think about exit strategies as a risk management process or asset protection in the investments they make in the business. Beyond the possible abrupt reasons—like the death or health-related examples above—what if you or they discover a stronger market opportunity or an advantageous and immediate suitor? Without adequate foresight and appropriate planning, you could easily leave behind a mess of a business—one that is poorly maintained with little or no appropriate record keeping and missing information for critical decision points or, worse yet, one that may have to go through liquidation or a "fire sale" to pay back its investors. In a change-of-control scenario, you could easily leave money on the table. If you have any aspirations of retiring, there is a good chance you'll need the proceeds of that sale. An exit strategy can help you make the transition smooth and the payout profitable. Rest assured your investors are going to think in this manner.

Regardless of the reasons you choose to exit—personal, professional, or financial—how you exit and the planning process you follow can have a profound impact on all areas listed above. The exit planning and, when necessary, the execution of the plan also greatly affect the relationships most important to you—those with your business and financial partners, employees, customers, suppliers, and even your family and loved ones outside the office.

Three fundamental topics are at stake:

1. Why to exit
2. How to exit
3. When to exit

Why to Exit: Where Am I?

You have to start the process by being candid and specific with yourself about why you are leaving your business. Savvy entrepreneurs are very honest with themselves and seek advice from people whom they respect. You should plot your exit strategy and talk it through with trusted advisors from the very first day you accept outside funding.

Most entrepreneurs are generalists. They are very good at being able to change who they are. There will come a time as the company grows that it outgrows them, personally or professionally. Unfortunately, in many cases, others see it coming long before the entrepreneur is willing to admit it. Lots of entrepreneurs try to change who they are, but if you are honest with yourself, your investors will gain confidence.

The reasons for exiting set the stage in preparation of the right kind of exit strategy most suitable for your business, industry, and point in the company's evolution. It will help identify the appropriate people, how to involve them in your plans, and—just as crucial—the time frame to put key processes in motion. Your reasons will also play a fundamental role in the deal structure when you accept outside capital if you plan to sell the business or transition it to someone else to run it.

Does your reason for leaving really matter? Actually, yes, it does. Think about it: if you plan to sell the business to cash in on everyone's investment, your exit strategy will include steps to exit the business at the right time to achieve the best price. Conversely, if you plan to exit by handing your business over to a successor, your strategy must include a carefully thought out succession planning process to prepare the most appropriate short list of candidates to take the helm. Remember that your exit strategy should also allow for sufficient investment of time and effort to transition your key relationships—often your most valuable asset—to others within the organization.

Sometimes the rationale to exit a business is obvious, such as retirement, health reasons, or, ideally, an offer to sell on the table that is too good to pass up. Whatever your reasons, a successful transition game plan begins by getting in touch with what's driving you to exit the business.

Below is a list of the most common reasons for exiting a business. How did your answers in exercise 8.1 compare to these?

Exercise 8.1
Why Exit a Business?

Follow these two quick steps to help you narrow down why you're trying to exit the business.

Step 1: Anticipate your reasons for exiting. Pretend your life is on a DVD. Fast-forward to the chapter where you're at a dinner gathering and you are describing to friends how you successfully exited your business. Summarize what you're telling them here:

_____

_____

Step 2: Prioritize your reasons.

_____

_____

_____

- "I'm burned out. I don't have the enthusiasm I once had for this business."
- "I'm bored. I need more of a challenge."
- "My investors are forcing me out."
- "I'm not as successful as I want to be."
- "I want to start another business, and I need to cash out of this one."
- "I want more time to spend with my spouse and family or on other things that interest me, such as nonprofit commitments or teaching at a local university."
- "I want to relocate to another geographic area."
- "I want to leave the business to my child as my successor."
- "My health is causing me to leave the business."
- "I'm ready to retire."
- "My business won't continue to prosper on its own. It needs to combine with other businesses to really thrive."
- "This business is successful now, and I want to cash out while things are going so well and the market conditions are good."
- "I've had several offers, and I plan to take the next really good one."

How to Exit: What Do I Want?

Once you have acknowledged your reasons for exiting, the best way to begin the planning phase is to be proactive. An exit, similar to the "closing" stage of a sale, should be a logical next step in the evolution of the business. The worst approach would be to wait until the business is in trouble and selling is your only way out—which is what happened to a lot of dot-com companies during the 1999–2001 bubble. Think of the exit as an opportunity to achieve the goals you've tied to your reasons for leaving. This is a chance to think about the best approach for a transition or a sale of that which you and others have worked so hard to build.

The difference between a transition—transferring the day-to-day management of your business to (ideally) a handpicked successor—and the sale of your business to a third party can significantly affect what you receive from the process and your role in the business moving forward. The range varies. It might be, "Thanks very much, here's your check—take care." It might mean remaining passively involved as an advisor. Or it might mean remaining active as an equity owner or board member with a high degree of influence in the future evolution of the business. In the latter case, if the incoming leadership continues to grow the business, it can potentially provide an ongoing earning stream through your equity position in the business.

Sell the business outright, and you'll trade ownership (and often any level of influence and type of involvement in the business moving forward) in exchange for a pot of gold. Taking outside investments adds a level of complexity because your exit will more than likely become a group decision—such as that of a board. Depending on the specific terms of the transaction, you may retain financial interest in the firm.

"Should I stay or should I go?" is a question that many exiting entrepreneurs struggle with—personally and professionally. Smart investors and buyers often make their offers contingent on continued participation and contribution by the founder or key managers of the business. This is often reflected in a "vesting schedule" of your stock options or an "earn-out," whereby you earn the cash value of a portion of the equity you sold over some period of time and based on achieving specific results. This helps to ensure continuity of operations, ensures that key employee and customer relationships do not end abruptly, and lowers the overall risk of the purchase.

One good litmus test is whether the valuation or sale price of your business heavily depends on forecasted future sales or product development. If so, it is more common for key selling or development resources (often the owner) to stay connected with the company. Many investors and buyers retain central people as advisors, consultants, or board members.

Two other quick points for your consideration: First, when a partnership is dissolved, one person usually keeps the company and the others are typically paid for their shares. Unless you have decided in advance which person stays and which are paid, the business may suffer significant and even irreparable damage due to the legal entanglements that arise from a hostile business transition. Furthermore, the stakeholders might not be entitled to equal shares of the company. Talk with your attorney about drafting legal documents that detail the division of the company and its assets. If you do raise outside capital, these issues will be clearly spelled out in the term sheet.

Second, if you are operating a small, closely held business, the line between business and personal assets can often be blurred. Disentangling which assets are which at the end of any business's life cycle is a hardship no entrepreneur (or those left behind) needs to endure. A much better approach is to incorporate the business and create and maintain a consistent asset management system. As such, investors will require the business to become a limited liability corporation (LLC) or a C corporation before committing their capital. Consult your attorney and accountant for more information.

Exercise 8.2
Selecting Your Exit Strategy

One of the best avenues to creating your exit strategy is to explore the paths previously laid by others, determine the key influencers, and then select the best path for your personal and professional situation.

Step 1: Prioritize the most common exit strategies. From the most commonly used exit strategies listed below, choose the one that most applies to you. Or, if you have another one in mind, write it in the space provided below.

- Sell/transition the business and play no future role in it.
- Sell/transition the business while keeping an active role in its operations.
- Transition management of the business to a handpicked successor, such as a family member.
- Hire/appoint a professional manager to manage the business, maintaining your ownership.
- Sell the business to your employees.
- Liquidate the business by selling its assets, terminating all employees, and closing the doors.

Step 2: What are the key influencers of your exit strategy? It's more practical to think about your exit strategy in terms of your personal and professional goals, as well as the nature of the business you're running. Answer the following questions to help develop an exit strategy that's appropriate for you:

- *My personal role.* To what extent do I personally want to continue working in the business? What tasks and activities (setting strategy, marketing and sales, financial management, operations, etc.) do I want to stay involved in? Do I want any future role at all? If asked to stay on as part of the sale or transition, would I be willing to do so? For how long?

- *Customer relationships.* To what extent is continued customer support and loyalty to the business an important consideration? Will the business perpetuate my name or reputation after I exit? Does the choice of successor or buyer include considerations of how certain customers will be treated? Is this a major concern or issue that could be a deal breaker?

(continued)

Exercise 8.2 (*continued*)

- *Financial return (for you and or your investors).* To what extent is achieving maximum return from the sale of the business a key consideration? If I had to choose between selling at a lower price to someone who would grow the business on the same path I've established or selling at a higher price to someone who would change the focus and direction of the company, whom would I choose? Am I willing to be patient with the sale to obtain the best price? Am I willing to make tough decisions about choosing a successor who has the management skills required to keep/make the business financially successful?

_____

_____

- *Other stakeholders.* To what extent is protecting and furthering the interests of stakeholders in the business a key consideration? Do I need those with an interest in my business to approve my exit strategy before I move forward?

_____

_____

- *Sense of urgency.* To what extent is it critical that my exit strategy be implemented and completed immediately or in the very short term? Are there considerations of health, finances, or other factors that compel an immediate exit, or can I afford to carry out the strategy over an extended time frame? Is the extended time frame best measured in months or years? To what extent is the selling price or selling attractiveness of the business dependent on a market-driven window of opportunity? If planning to transition the business to a successor (family, employee, or group) as my exit strategy, how soon will that successor be ready?

_____

_____

Step 3: Select a strategy that best fits your situation. Review your answers in the first two steps and identify the best match for your situation. Describe that exit in a short paragraph.

_____

_____

_____

When to Exit: What Does My Plan Look Like?

Having prioritized the primary reason(s) and crafted a strategy, the next step is to determine an appropriate timeline for implementing your exit plan. Due to a true sense of urgency, some plans require an immediate plan of action—as in a quote from one investor conference call I participated in: "We need to announce the CEO change tomorrow!" If you have a longer leeway in terms of time, you can more effectively prepare and efficiently execute.

Should you ever plan for an immediate exit? If you plan to raise outside capital, investors will demand it. If you plan to sell your business, you will need time to clean up your operations and financial records, determine the appropriate valuation, identify appropriate and interested parties, and negotiate the deal—not to mention plan a smooth transition. If you plan to transition to a successor, you will need to carefully outline the most critical attributes of the company's next captain, identify potential internal candidates, explore external options if necessary, assess the right fit, and get them on board in the new role as you transition yourself out.

An immediate exit might be appropriate in the following circumstances:

- You need to remove yourself from the business for health reasons.
- You receive the fabled "offer I can't refuse."
- Your business is failing and the best thing to do is close the doors and sell the assets.
- The right successor is available and you realize that you've overstayed your usefulness or have lost all enthusiasm for running the business.

What if your plans don't include you leaving the business? I've spoken with several entrepreneurs who are deeply passionate about what they do. To them, it really is much more than a job. They're very good at it and are nowhere near retirement—many wouldn't know how to retire! If you're one of these people, you're probably asking yourself, "Do I still need an exit strategy?" The answer is still yes.

Your passion, your level of expertise, or how young you may be at heart still does not address a simple fact: you need to mitigate risk and preserve your investment if something unexpected happens to you. Your employees, customers, suppliers, and even family need a continuity and business disaster recovery plan if you're not there. It is critical that you get serious about this now and conduct an internal audit of your personal disability, key personal insurance policies, and management succession plans.

Exercise 8.3
Selecting Your Exit Time Frame

Your unique characteristics and the demands of the exit will guide your particular time frame. You might need a rapid execution to take advantage of another opportunity or have a lot of time to prepare your business for a transition or a sale. Let's review and document the appropriate time frame.

Step 1: Select your appropriate time frame. Think about the strategy you described in exercise 8.2. Review your notes and choose the time frame below that best fits your unique strategy:

- *Immediate:* My exit strategy requires that I exit my business as soon as possible. I need to develop an exit plan immediately.
- *Short-term:* My exit strategy requires that I sell/transition the business in a matter of a few months. I need to start working on an exit plan now and begin implementing it within the next 6–12 months.
- *Medium-term:* My chosen exit strategy allows me to exit my business in the next 12–24 months. I'll begin planning for sale or transition of my business in the near future.

(*continued*)

Exercise 8.3 (*continued*)

- *Long-term:* Some of the steps in my exit strategy will take a while to complete. My exit plans are in the "idea stage" now. I'll move toward action planning at a future point when I feel more ready.
- *Indefinite:* I don't plan to exit my business in the foreseeable future, but I need a contingency plan just in case I have to exit involuntarily.
- *Other:*

Step 2: "Map" your exit time frame. It's important that you use your answer above to develop a roadmap of the critical milestones ahead. With the end in mind, work backwards to determine the critical path to get you there. Write your schedule and recap:

- your exit time frame,
- your sense of urgency to get started,
- the target date for developing your exit plans

What Now?

Hopefully, through the three exercises in this chapter on why, how, and when to exit, you now have a good framework for your unique exit strategy plan. I would encourage you to use the framework you have developed here to identify other areas where you still have questions. The next step is to meet with a financial advisor, your accountant, your lawyer, and, if appropriate, a business consultant to ask each of them about the questions for which you still need answers.

It is also vitally important that you discuss your exit strategy plan with your family and close personal friends before raising outside capital. Your loved ones are often a great sounding board and will provide the most candid and straightforward advice you're likely to receive on your ideas and plans.

SUMMARY

☑ Valuing a business is both an art and a science that uses particular tools to value the worth of a company's hard and soft assets.

☑ Acquisitions require due diligence and the integration of unique yet (hopefully) synergistic cultures or market positions.

☑ Exit strategies pave the road for the next chapter in the owner's life and in the life cycle of the company.

☑ Valuation is particularly useful when estimating the value of alternative business strategies, assessing major transactions, conducting a value-based management review of operational performance, or communicating with key stakeholders.

☑ Two basic approaches to valuation: discounted cash flow (DCF) valuation and relative valuation.

☑ Strategic alliances or mergers and acquisitions (M&A), although an attractive growth strategy for certain businesses, create complexities and extensive costs of integration for smaller companies.

☑ A successful acquisition strategy encompasses critical and candid reasons for wanting the business you're thinking of buying. You should have a multitude of options, buy for quality, use the best transaction team you can afford, and preempt possible areas the merged company could fail in advance of the transaction.

☑ Many entrepreneurs don't have an adequate exit strategy.

☑ Why, how, and when to exit are critical questions with a multitude of options, all of which need to be carefully considered with personal and professional advisors.

9

Value-Added Financial Intermediaries

"Financial intermediaries," as they are often referred to, are the deal facilitators of any financing transaction. Whether called *advisors, brokers, consultants,* or *investment* or *merchant bankers*, they connect business people to sources of capital where it is needed or wanted. But remember: Very few happen to be your relatives, and they seldom work for free. Develop a vested interest in these people for your long-term success, and align their personal and professional objectives with those of your company's growth strategy.

SEEKING PROFESSIONAL FUNDRAISING HELP

When do you bring in these professionals? Interestingly, many entrepreneurs we spoke with recommended that you hire them, as one put it, "as soon as you have a problem—and sooner rather than later." There are three common events that trigger a call to outside fundraising professionals:

1. *A change in the business itself.* Usually a change for the better, this may include a planned acquisition or purchase of a building. An example is that of an entrepreneur I knew who wanted to buy "his" division from his large employer and run it as a spin-off business. Although not a large transaction, it was a complex one. As mentioned in earlier chapters, smaller banks are often most appropriate for smaller deals, but the complexity of this situation made the use of a larger bank a better decision—with a merchant banker shepherding the deal and directing the entrepreneur to the proper lender.
2. *A change in the current financial partnership.* When there is management change in the current funding source, the entrepreneur may lose confidence in the source's knowledge of (or interest in) his or her business. Poor client service, response delays, or increased requests for documentation may exacerbate this situation. One example of such a change in a business that created a change in the financial relationship was that of a $20 million company whose financial situation changed from a cash-flow-supported basis to an asset-intensive one when it heavily invested its cash in a new plant. Although the CEO and CFO knew all the right

bankers, they no longer fit their banking criteria and needed a different type of lender. The company's financial consultant was able to identify the right contacts and explain the market realities of asset-based lending.

3. *A change in the economy.* Entrepreneurs can be buffeted by major swings in the economy or drastic changes in market forces, any of which can affect their financial well-being. Think of the changes in the real estate market in 2007–2008.

The advantage an experienced consultant or banker offers can be likened to the value an insurance agent brings to the table. With intimate knowledge of several carriers, an agent can often do a better job finding you insurance than you could on your own. But just as a bad insurance agent will probably get you bad insurance, a bad financing consultant will likely get you undesirable financing.

If you've never raised capital before and don't fully understand the issues, hiring a financial intermediary is a wise move. If you are trying to raise a first round, for example, don't shop the deal to death and risk being overexposed—get help. It doesn't have to be an investment bank. There are people out there who have done this before and who are there to help, at least to get a company a fair chance to be heard. At the end of the day, if it's not investable, it's not investable—that won't change. But sometimes, it's a matter of getting in front of the right investors. The success of the two should be tied closely together.

One entrepreneur I interviewed was selling his $20 million manufacturing business to his daughter and son-in-law. Senior debt was the cheapest source of capital, so finding the right banker was important. However, with a limited amount of equity in the business, the owner needed another layer of capital—mezzanine financing. The challenge was that if the owner took on too much debt, the bank would still need to be paid back even if the company wasn't profitable. Equity financing, although more patient, would expect a significant return. This entrepreneur didn't know who could provide which type of financing, or if it would be at a fair price, and so he engaged a financial consultant.

Business owners who plan to buy a competitor most likely need similar help. They seldom know what their expectations should be, or whether debt, equity, or a combination best suits their needs.

"Buyer beware" is the first rule of hiring fundraising "experts" to help you raise capital. While there are plenty of qualified financial intermediaries out there, in truth just about anybody can (and, frighteningly, does) hang out a shingle, offering to write your business plan and introduce you to "potential" investors.

Where Do You Need Help?

Before you begin your search for financial intermediaries to help raise capital, it's critical to break the process down and really think through your personal strengths, your internal resources (if any), and the specific areas in which you need help. Specificity drives credibility. If you get very explicit about what type of help you may need, you're much more likely to find the right resource. More importantly, you'll have a clear expectation of what help you'll need, options for comparison shopping of similar services, and a range of appropriate types and amounts of compensation.

Here are some of the processes to consider:

1. *Cleaning your house.* Have entrepreneurs who have raised capital before come in and "audit" your business, specifically for:
   - financial order
   - operating efficiency
   - sales and revenue effectiveness
   - believability of the present "story"
   - promise of the future "potential"
2. *Business plan writing.* The fundraising process can often be as much about marketing as it is about operations and financial analysis. You're trying to sell your story and the promise and potential of investing in it. Preparing a business plan—see figure 9.1 for the four basic approaches—is an important step for any business, but it's vital when securing financing. For that reason, many business owners hire consultants to help them research, organize, and present all of the relevant business plan information to potential investors. The most important factors to consider when comparing consultants are:
   - Experience: How many business plans have they written in total?
   - Success: What percentage of the plans they've written have been funded?
   - Cost: Do they charge by the job or the hour? Paying a per-project fee may be more economical than an hourly fee.
3. *Introduction to funding sources.* Even with the best plans, you need highly personal and credible introductions to funding sources. The bigger your need, the higher the profile of the individuals you'll need introductions to. Smart attorneys, accountants, bankers, consultants, and even executive recruiters, in an effort to earn your business in these areas, are often willing to introduce you to their investor relationships.
4. *Due diligence support.* Once you've identified an interested party, they're going to want to dive deep into your financials, operations, technology, customers, sales efforts, legal and financial structure, and more. If you don't have the capability or the knowledge, you'll need some help. Think of this process as something similar to an IRS audit.
5. *Financing terms and conditions.* Unless they're extremely astute in finance, this is where most entrepreneurs get in trouble. You need a very sharp CFO and corporate attorney, experienced in having raised capital, to advise you independently as to the terms and conditions you're agreeing to.

Where and How to Begin Looking for Outside Help

Since the dawn of business, where to look for quality financial intermediaries has been a challenge. Here are some sources and options to consider as you begin to search for the right resources in those areas where you need most help.

Figure 9.1
The Four Basic Approaches to Preparing a Business Plan

You have four basic approaches to preparing your business plan:
1. *Prepare it yourself the old-fashioned way.* This means scouring Web sites and reading books to learn about how to prepare a business plan.
2. *Prepare it yourself using business planning software.* Most software packages cost less than $100. They guide you through the process by asking you a series of questions about your business.
3. *Hire an inexpensive business plan consultant to write the plan for you.* Caveat emptor. You get what you pay for.
4. *Hire an excellent business plan consultant to write the plan for you.* Again, you get what you pay for—which, if you do your homework, can be top quality.

The advantages and disadvantages of each of these methods are as follows:

Strategy	Advantages	Disadvantages	Comments
Do it yourself *without* software	• Costs relatively little (the price of a few books). • Many free outlines can be found on the Web. • Can be a great way to think through the many issues facing a young venture. • Will force you to learn about subjects that fall outside of your core expertise, whether they be finance, marketing, sales, risk management, product planning, or competitor analysis.	• Very expensive in terms of your time, especially if you do not have a strong business and financial background. • Mistakes can be very costly, especially if you are seeking equity funding. • If you're not a good writer, you'll have to find a good editor.	• This is probably most appropriate for an "idea business plan" or an operating business plan that will not be shown to investors.

Figure 9.1 (*continued*)

Do it yourself *with* software	• Relatively inexpensive. • Some software comes with sample business plans for many industries that you can use as a starting point. • The rigid structure makes sure that you don't leave out anything important.	• Most software packages are not very flexible. • The result looks "cookie cutter." • You still have to write all of the text yourself, so if you're not a good writer, you'll have to find a good editor. • Still quite time consuming, although less so than doing it without software	• This option may be appropriate if you plan to start a low-tech business like a restaurant or a store and are seeking bank or possibly even angel funding. • You should be very wary about using this plan for venture capital or corporate investors, since a poorly written business plan will blow the only chance you have.
Hire an *inexpensive* business plan consultant	• Relatively inexpensive (under $5,000, and sometimes even under $1,000). • Saves you time. • Quick turnaround times.	• Most mass produce business plans using business planning software. They ask you a series of canned questions, fill in the blanks in the software, and send you the results with little or no value-added consulting. You are essentially paying them to type your responses into the software for you. • Many are part-timers who have never started a business themselves. • More often than not, the business plan will require a complete rewrite if you plan to seek equity funding	• Same comments as above. If you are lucky, you may find one of the few inexpensive consultants who produce reasonably good results

(continued)

Hire an *excellent* business plan consultant		

- The best consultants have written many plans that have raised capital, and they understand what investors want to see.
- You can save literally hundreds of hours—which you can spend building your business.
- Can generate value-added ideas in all areas, and can help you position your company for success.
- They provide an objective outside perspective and will challenge your assumptions.
- They perform independent market and competitor research.

- Fairly expensive (usually well over $10,000).
- It can be difficult to distinguish between the excellent and the average business plan consultant (*hint*: look at their track records).

- If you are preparing an equity funding plan and you have never written a funded plan before, you should give this option serious consideration.
- Even if you know how to write a plan, you should be devoting your time to building your business.
- The business plan is often the only basis a potential investor has to decide whether or not to invite you to their office for that all-important first meeting. If you need medical attention, you hire a good doctor. If you need a contract, you hire a good lawyer. So, if a business plan is critical to your success, why wouldn't you hire the best consultant you can find?

- *Go where they gather.* Organizations such as the Association for Corporate Growth (ACG) or the Turnaround Management Association (TMA) are common ground for investment bankers, mergers-and-acquisitions advisors, financial and operating consultants, and others generally involved in the financial transactions industry. Many of these organizations have annual conferences that serve not only as great opportunities to learn about the industry but also as the place to meet legitimate and value-added providers.
- *Read what they subscribe to on- and off-line.* Dealmaker, Merger Mania, and other similar publications not only offer insightful articles about the capital-raising process, case studies, and best practices but also mention key individuals and firms involved. Several Web sites are also particularly useful in identifying key financial intermediaries.
- *Credibility by association.* Many entrepreneurs I interviewed mentioned that their existing portfolios of service-provider relationships—banker, accountant, lawyer, operations consultants, or extended friends—were by far the best sources for identifying financial intermediaries.
- *Get free help from the government.* Believe it or not, the U.S. government wants small businesses to thrive, and it has several agencies and partnerships established for that exact purpose. Two services that provide free or low-cost business plan preparation help are the Small Business Administration's (SBA) Small Business Development Centers (SBDCs) and the Service Corps of Retired Executives (SCORE).

   According to its Web site, the SBDC "provides management assistance to current and prospective small business owners." SBDCs offer one-stop assistance to individuals and small businesses by providing a wide variety of information and guidance in central and easily accessible branch locations. The program is a cooperative effort of the private sector, the educational community, and federal, state, and local governments and is an integral component of Entrepreneurial Development's network of training and counseling services.

   SCORE, "Counselors to America's Small Business," is a nonprofit association resource partner of the SBA, dedicated to educating entrepreneurs and the formation, growth, and success of small business nationwide. At its 389 chapters throughout the United States and its territories, 10,500 working and retired executives and business owners volunteer their time and expertise as business counselors.
- *Find consultants specializing in your type of business.* A good way to whittle down your options is to find those financial intermediaries who specialize in your industry and in businesses of your size. You can search for these consultants at www.guru.com and www.bplans.com or consult the directory at www.business.com.

Considerations in Engaging Outside Help

The ideal fee structure with consultants is a modest monthly retainer with a success fee, usually a percentage of the capital raised or, more often for smaller deals, an equity stake in the company on the back end.

Contingency arrangements may save fees, but here are three ways they typically fail:

1. If prolonged effort is required, consultants may run out of steam.
2. They may be tempted to push a certain transaction not because it's in the best interest of your business or particular situation, but because it's the fastest route to the closing table and obtaining their back-end fee.
3. Entrepreneurs tend not to take the advice of professionals they are not paying. This can cause the consultant to become prematurely discouraged and lead to the collapse of the relationship.

According to National Association of Securities Dealers regulations, a person must pass the General Securities Representative Exam, commonly referred to as the Series 7 Exam, to become a registered representative of an investment broker-dealer in the United States. In the case of a public offering, investment bankers sometimes refuse to pay intermediaries because it reduces the amount of compensation they can earn from a deal. Likewise, in some private transactions, investors prefer to not pay off a financial intermediary. Experienced consultants know this and shop their deals to sources of capital that protect their fees. But it doesn't always work out this way. Consultants often end up working with investors they've never met before. Situations can get sticky, with the entrepreneur actually mediating between the would-be investor and his or her own consultants.

You can avoid many of the problems of equity compensation by having consultants buy their equity cheaply before the search for capital begins. Of course, if the consultants don't produce, you may have unwanted, and sometimes cantankerous, minority shareholders. The whole process is structurally imperfect and, as a result, plain old fees are sometimes the best way to go.

Here are some other considerations in hiring consultants:

- *Out-clauses are important.* Make sure there is a sixty-day out-clause in your contract. If you aren't put in contact with investors within this time frame, your deal is probably withering.
- *Checking references is a must.* It's amazing how many entrepreneurs hire consultants without looking into their pasts. To check their references, speak to the principals of three firms the consultant has worked for. Did the consultant add value? Did he do what he said he would? Did she act professionally? Most importantly, did the consultant raise the money needed?
- *Check out their staff and find out who will be responsible for helping you prepare your plan.* Will the work be done by an experienced entrepreneur with an MBA or a junior consultant just getting started? Many "About Us" sections of most legitimate firm Web sites will provide you with a glimpse of the talent pool you'll be working with.
- *Spread your net wide.* Although working with someone locally can be convenient, don't limit yourself solely to consultants within a five-mile

radius. The best one for you may be a few hundred miles away or even across the country.

- *Examine work samples.* Besides cost, one of the ways to differentiate firms is through their work. Ask to see samples of completed plans to get a sense of the firm's style and capabilities. Some firms allow you to skim samples of their work online, such as at the Business Plan Store or at www.masterplanz.com, although many prefer to provide them off-line.
- *Outsource the function, not the results.* Even if you outsource the writing of your plan to someone else, be sure you stay involved in the process so that you can answer detailed questions from potential investors later. It still needs to be *your* plan.
- *Optimize the necessary time and effort.* The more work you can do up front to gather statistics, organize your background materials, or create a first draft, the less time a consultant has to spend on the project, potentially reducing the amount of your final bill.

As is often the case, leveraging an existing (or previous) business network and asking for referrals from trusted business acquaintances may be the best way to identify the most relevant financial intermediary for your particular situation. Following that with the above outlined due-diligence investigation about the intermediary's previous engagements and successes, supplemented by a more instinctual or "gut-level" feeling about their ability to develop a relationship of trust, should result in a good selection.

Although some financial intermediaries prefer to be paid on a consulting basis, it is more common to set a retainer and then pay on the basis of successful accomplishment of the deal. It is not uncommon for the intermediary to expect an exclusive relationship, similar to that of a real estate listing agent.

THE ART OF RAISING CAPITAL

Even with the support of a financial intermediary, you will discover that there is a definite art to raising capital. The most valuable financial intermediaries should also serve as sounding boards for very fundamental questions you need to ask of yourself and them—before you embark on a challenging, time- and resource-intensive, and distracting process. The really savvy intermediaries will not only reduce their self-interest to develop and nurture a lasting relationship with you but also disarm you with their candor and appeal to your logical self-interest. Said another way, even though they may want your consulting, legal, or accounting business, the really good ones will not take on a project if they're not confident they'll succeed, rather than taking it on simply for the fees and failing in the ultimate funding success.

What's Their Litmus Test?

An interesting early interaction with a financial intermediary is to gauge how much value they add in every interaction *before* you engage them.

I'm not talking about expecting free work or abusing a prospective long-term financial partner, but about looking for unique insights or perspectives that you may not have thought of previously or received elsewhere.

One solid example of their vested interest is the early discussions of whether your particular business is fundable by outside investors. Again, the really strong intermediaries have seen it all and should have a solid grasp of various investment sources' expectations, the respective investor's sweet spot (preferences in funding size, duration, industry, and so on), their due-diligence process, and the required effort to get a business funded.

Bill Reichert, managing director of Garage Technology Ventures, has invested in companies that have raised $750 million in angel and venture capital funding in the past decade. He reinforces this point as being fundamental to your efforts with any outside help. Does it really make sense for you to go out and pound your head against the wall in the capital market to try to raise money? The harsh reality, which many entrepreneurs candidly don't want to hear, is that not every brilliant idea is fundable. There are a lot of really good ideas—there are even a lot of really good companies—that really should not be going after institutional capital, because, as mentioned earlier, professional capital (such as venture capital or private equity) is expensive, it's distracting from your core competency of running the business, and it will fundamentally change the dynamics of your business in management and governance.

Outside capital is going to look for rapid growth and a clearly sustainable differentiation that will drive ongoing, "consistently disproportionate profitability," according to Bill. So, if you believe your business is fundable, the next conversation with any financial intermediary is about how to best raise outside capital. Pay particular attention to the process advisors outline and look for the following four critical success factors:

1. *Did you start smart?* Successful fundraising down the road is directly related to the questions financial intermediaries should ask you around how you began the business and the progress you've made thus far. The devil is very much in the details here, so as they aim to put your "story" together for presentation to prospective investors, they need to be able to not only regurgitate it but to defend it!
2. *Can you tell a good story?* Forget fundraising for a second. Can you generally tell a compelling, interesting, engaging story—say, at a dinner table with a group of personal friends? How about your financial intermediaries—can they understand the fundamentals of your business, beyond putting together good-looking slides? With your help, they really have to understand the details, internalize them, and be able to articulate them—ideally with conviction and credibility. For example, do your numbers add up? There is a great deal of economics in every business, and the ability to succinctly articulate and defend those will be crucial to your success.
3. *What does their playbook look like?* I can't emphasize enough how much this is *not* a "seat of the pants" approach. If you meet a financial

intermediary who likes to "wing it," run—don't walk, run! Anyone who offers his or her professional services should have a very specific process for being successful in finding the right investors for your company.

4. *Can you build and protect your credibility?* Intermediaries, prospective investors, customers, suppliers, employees, and industry thought leaders are all part of a unique, often highly integrated ecosystem. Building and nurturing your credibility on a consistent basis with this entire group—through performance and investment in key relationships—will be critical to your successful fundraising efforts.

How Long Should the Process Take?

Most entrepreneurs vastly underestimate the commitment of time and effort necessary to successfully complete a financing round. As a general rule of thumb, a company seeking financing needs to budget between 500 to 1,000 person-hours to their fundraising process, spread out over a six- to nine-month period (sometimes twelve to eighteen, depending on the size and complexity of the fundraising effort).

Consider the following five critical steps in the process:

1. Perfecting the business plan, offering memorandum, and other due-diligence materials
2. Developing a comprehensive, highly targeted, and relevant prospective investor list
3. Contacting this list multiple times and responding to a multitude of investor due-diligence requests
4. Scheduling and conducting various interactions such as entrepreneur and investor calls and in-person presentations
5. Negotiating the transaction

Just taking the first step, completing the business plan, typically requires at least 200 hours of work. This time is dedicated to conducting the market research to validate the opportunity, developing a comprehensive financial model, determining the most effective way to lay out the business strategy, and actually writing and proofing the business plan.

The next step, developing a comprehensive and highly relevant targeted prospective investor list, is also time consuming. There are thousands of potential investors, each of which has very different preferences regarding the types of ventures that interest them. Some invest by market sector (e.g., health care or telecommunications), stage (seed stage or later stages), geography, or a combination of these factors. Many hours must be dedicated to determining which investors are the right fit for the respective business owner. This process involves creating a master investor list, visiting each investor's Web site to view investment criteria and past investments, and choosing the right contact at the target firm.

To see how easily the time adds up, consider that only about 25 percent of prospective investors who show initial interest in a transaction actually progress to detailed company due diligence. From there, only about 10 percent of this preliminary group actually continue to a legitimate letter of intent or offer of funds, of which only 25 percent actually result in an investment transaction. As such, completing a financing transaction requires, on average, contacting approximately 150 to 200 prequalified prospective investors.

The due-diligence process, in which investors scrutinize the investment, can also be time-consuming for the company. Investors often request many documents, some of which can be easily retrieved from files (e.g., prior tax returns), while others may take considerable time to prepare specially (additional market analysis, customer lists with past purchases, contact information, etc.). Scheduling phone calls, webinars, and in-person meetings between the entrepreneurs and the investors often takes extensive logistical planning, not to mention the entrepreneur's preparation time for the investor presentations.

Finally, negotiating a transaction can take a significant amount of time depending upon the complexity of the transaction and number of parties involved. Financial intermediaries often have to coordinate discussions among numerous accounting and legal teams.

Too many companies fail to raise capital because they are unaware of the significant time requirements in doing so. Those firms who understand these requirements and budget accordingly are the ones most likely to persevere and end up with the capital they need and the most relevant financial partners they desire.

It's a Relationship Business

The best client–intermediary relationships are based on an exceptional level of candor and trust that reflects the credibility of both parties. Entrepreneurs should expect their intermediary to demonstrate integrity, creativity, proven problem-solving skills, and a passion for their business and what they are doing for them. Likewise, intermediaries expect their clients to be forthcoming and timely with critical information, responsive to various other requests, focused on consistent performance during the fundraising process, and open to learning and growing (personally and professionally) during this journey. To many, it also really helps to have the entrepreneurs check their egos at the door—particularly if they're new to the fundraising process, despite their past professional success.

The financial intermediaries wear a lot of hats—some of them surprising. The best of the breed are counselors, business consultants, and advocates for the client company. "You may want to set another place at the Thanksgiving table, because the right intermediary will almost feel like a member of the family," commented Penny Hulbert, principal of Links Financial LLC and president of the Tampa Bay Chapter of the Association for Corporate Growth.

SUMMARY

☑ Financial intermediaries such as consultants, brokers, and investment and merchant bankers aim to facilitate financial transactions by connecting sources of capital to where they are needed or wanted the most.

☑ Changes in the business, the financial partnership between entrepreneurs and their investors, and the economy are the three most common events for engaging a financial intermediary.

☑ Before one begins the search for financial intermediaries to help raise capital, it's critical to break the process down and really think through one's personal strengths, internal resources (if any), and specific areas in need of external help.

☑ Business audits, gap analyses of the current company position compared to that which is expected by the investor community, business plan development, introductions to potential investors, due-diligence support, and negotiating the transaction are some of the areas of expertise by financial intermediaries.

☑ Government sources, industry insiders, other entrepreneurs who have raised capital, and general business colleagues are often good sources of introductions to intermediaries.

☑ Appropriate fee structures, extensive due diligence of their past work, reference checking, and out-clauses are recommended approaches to engaging a financial intermediary.

☑ The art of raising capital includes getting a smart start, telling a compelling story, having a solid playbook, and developing your credibility within the fundraising system.

☑ The fundraising process can take six to eighteen months or more.

☑ Fundraising is unquestionably a relationship business.

10

The Experts Speak: Best Practices to Embrace and Top Mistakes to Avoid

A mentor once told me that experience comes from making bad decisions. Wisdom comes from learning from other peoples' experiences. What would the entrepreneurs I interviewed have done differently if they had the chance to do it all over again? What painful and often expensive lessons did they learn that they would like to pass on to others embarking on this journey? What consistent mistakes do investors see entrepreneurs making over and over again? If there was a resource of "wish I knew" or "wish I could tell them to do" items for before, during, and after the fundraising process, what would it include?

I WISH I KNEW THEN ...

This chapter provides the results I got when I asked my interviewees these questions. To protect the identity of the innocent, I've excluded the sources. According to my experts, there are several mistakes to avoid before you begin raising capital. Most of the comments I received fell into one of three time frames:

- Before you begin the process
- During the fundraising campaign
- After you have accepted their money

Many answers are straightforward, and every one resulted in gray or lost hairs for the courageous souls who proudly call themselves entrepreneurs and show up every morning to make a difference. Where multiple ideas were shared under the same general heading—perhaps from an entrepreneur and an investor's perspective—I've included both.

Separately, I noticed that several entrepreneurs and investors consistently referenced the same or similar publications and Web sites and introduced some great tools. Successful fundraising is a moving target, and as a lifelong learner myself, I thought it would be useful to compile these resources in Appendix A, as the Ultimate Resource Library of 500+ favorite

Web sites and tools. I found each uniquely valuable, and several are applicable under separate categories in this book. Here is your opportunity to gain some wisdom from their experiences.

Visit http://www.relationshipeconomics.net/raisingcapital.html for the most up-to-date information.

Before You Begin the Process

Allowing the Process of Raising Capital to Become a Diversion

You should always recognize that raising capital is a diversion from what you *should* be doing. It will cost you twice as much and take twice as long. Even though you may fall in love with the process, the basic idea is this: Do it once, and move on with your life. The difference in the capital raising is not as great as the difference you can make in the business by focusing your time there.

Selling Securities Online

While you may be able to sell your personal belongings or even find a date online, any kind of advertising almost always violates securities laws. Both state and federal laws prohibit any kind of "general solicitation" for most kinds of private securities offerings.

Paying Employees for Help

One company offered its sales force a big commission check if they found and closed potential investors. One minor problem: under the securities laws, a company isn't permitted to pay anyone other than a licensed broker-dealer a commission or other success-based compensation in connection with the sale of its securities.

Going after Small Ideas

It's just as hard to create a company around a small idea as it is to create a company around a big idea. You might as well go after the biggest opportunity you possibly can with your business—it will be just as difficult to go after the smallest.

Ask yourself, What's the problem? Basically, if there isn't a big enough problem in the market—a major unfilled need—then there's no point in trying to sell a solution. How severe is the problem? An attractive problem, from the venture capitalist's (VC) point of view, is one that the market will collectively spend $1 billion or more to solve.

Fundraising without an Objective Self-analysis

Make sure you understand *why* you are raising capital. Look in the mirror and do the best you can to give yourself an objective self-analysis. What do we do well? What do we want to do? Why do we want this money, and how will we spend it? Do we want to buy another company? Do we have orders lined up so we need new equipment to fill these orders faster? Use a realistic filter. Ask yourself, What is the first step? When you raise this money, what is the first thing you will do when you get the money? You have to perform an objective self-analysis.

Lack of Focus

When raising capital, focus on these five things:

1. The management team: Build a management team so that you can move forward and so people can see the business and not just the product. The product is just a vehicle to get the money.
2. The market opportunity: Know what kind it is and, if it's a strong one, really outline that.
3. Business strategy: Build one that focuses on the investor and how the investor is going to get his or her money back.
4. Customers: Find customers who are buying the product.
5. Financials: Make sure yours are in order.

Somewhere down the line, tell the investors about your product, but focus on the business. Too many presentations focus on the product and not the strategy. There are three questions I always ask (usually answered in a positioning paper):

1. What are the problems in the industry?
2. What is different and better about what you do compared to what anyone else does?
3. Why does that difference matter?

It is very important that you can articulate these three things. I put a card in front of each of my clients that asks, "Whose job am I doing now?" I try to get them to stop working *in* the business and work *on* the business.

Raising Capital When You're in Trouble

A lot of companies decide, "We're in trouble. We just lost a huge client. Now we're burning $50,000 a month in salaries…" and so on. Those companies decide that they need growth capital, but this is not the time to do that. Instead, you need to find some new sales, cut costs, and so forth. Many companies decide to raise growth capital when they are in trouble— which is the worst time to do it. You will spend more time trying to raise money than fixing the business. Raise money *before* you need it, because when you need it, it will cost you a fortune.

Getting Left Behind

You may miss the window. We have seen many people with the best technology that haven't been able to raise the necessary capital to support the business moving forward. You may get stuck behind. Others have a lifestyle business and never realize the true market opportunity. The opportunity cost is a lifestyle business that can be sustainable for a few years but does not take advantage of market opportunity and accelerated growth.

Not Being Open to Strategic Options

You might be in a fast-moving market that is still fairly immature, and two years ago was like the Wild West. Now, it is starting to mature. In five years, there will be established players with market share. But right now, no one has a huge position in the market. You have to start ramping up soon if you want to become one of the top three players. Would you consider merging with someone to scale the business?

Trying to Fund a Moving Target

Behind the entire process of raising capital, there is a backdrop of economic liquidity. Transactions that were successful last year might be unsuccessful under identical terms next year. The environment is constantly moving; the players are constantly changing. Just as mortgage and insurance products are being developed daily, different approaches to raising capital and different techniques are emerging. Be current and well informed before you enter a deal.

Taking the Road Less Traveled—Alone

One mistake entrepreneurs make is that we think the capital-raising process is not that difficult and that it's what we're *supposed* to do. If you are doing something that you have not done before, enlist a consultant like an investment banker. If it is significant to your business and you have never done it—don't do it alone. It may be easy for the serial entrepreneur who can anticipate the roadblocks, but for a new entrepreneur, there will be decisions that have never been faced before. Expect that—don't think that you have all of the answers.

Not Accounting for Time to Profitability

When investors evaluate the potential investment value of a business, one of the most important factors they consider is how fast the company will be able to turn a profit. Speed to profitability is one of the consistently most predictive factors in determining the success of a company. If your business is on the slow track when it comes to profitability, your road to finding capital will be extremely rough.

Thinking that There Is No Competition

If you believe this to be true, then either there is no market for your product or your own due diligence has been weak. If you believe smarter teams with deeper pockets can't reverse-engineer your solution or drag out your patent for years to come while you run out of money, you're either extremely arrogant or short-sighted. None of this will bolster an investor's confidence.

What are the alternative solutions, and what makes yours the best? No matter what you may think, you *do* have competitors. If you've invented a teleporter that moves people from point A to point B, your competitors still include trains, planes, and automobiles (and bicycles and sneakers). What makes your solution better than the alternative solutions for getting from A to B?

Selling to the Wrong Investors

Even though an investor may meet the income or wealth guidelines required by law, it doesn't mean that it's in your best interest to sell that investor your company's securities. For example, in a private offering limited to accredited investors, a company can sell to anyone with more than $1 million in net assets. The problem is that, back when this law was written, $1 million in net assets was a substantial number. Now it's not uncommon for someone to have that much equity in a home.

Typically, it's the investors who are inexperienced in investing in start-up companies that are the most likely to complain to securities regulators or sue if they're not happy. And whether an investor's complaint has merit or not, dealing with a state investigation or lawsuit will take valuable resources away from the company and divert management's attention away from building the company.

Half-baked Business Plans

From an investor's perspective, there's nothing worse than entrepreneurs who walk into investor presentations unprepared. If you haven't put the time and energy into writing a well-thought-out, cohesive executive summary and supporting full-blown business plan, including the fundamental financial projections and a competitive market analysis, it will be a really short meeting! It reminds me of the *American Idol* or *America's Got Talent* auditions—"Thank you. Next!"

I probably see five to ten business plans a week. Frankly, most aren't ready for the big leagues. Entrepreneurs really need to figure out the formula or get some help in the process. They need to make it easier for investors to quickly see the value in a company. With start-up quality improving, investors have more to choose from. Now more than ever, it's important for a business plan to make the right first impression.

Engaging the Wrong Outside Help

Most consultants fail to help entrepreneurs raise capital because they don't take the time to really understand the business. To be successful, they must become almost like a member of the management team.

Focusing Too Much on the Idea and Too Little on the Management

"It wasn't enough for us to convince potential investors that we had invented the next killer mobile payment concept. What we lacked was the team to take our ideas to market and generate the revenues to repay a bank loan or show the probable exit strategies for a VC."

Why are *you* the best team to do this? You may have a great solution to a big problem, but you won't get others to invest if your team doesn't have the skills to execute your vision. What have you done, and what will you do? Ideas are a dime a dozen. Execution is what really counts. You need to show that you have the ability to make the right things happen. A good track record and aggressive future milestones (along with a realistic plan for making it happen) show that you mean business.

Not Raising Enough Money

"We started out with way too little money, and that really led to us having to shut the place down. We planned the best-case scenario and didn't raise enough to endure how long it took us to complete the product and get it out in the market. By the time we hired people, put developers on the right track, and started talking to customers, we had run out of cash and had few options left!"

How much do you need, and what will you do with the money? Investors want to know if the entrepreneur has a realistic understanding of the costs involved in starting and scaling his or her business.

During the Fundraising Campaign

Poor Packaging

Those entrepreneurs with the best chance of success are the ones who put together a very good package on the front end. When they go to investors, they understand what the investors are going to be looking for and have that information ready when they go in. These entrepreneurs include information on who they are, what they do, and what they're looking for, along with current financials and projection models. When you do that, your chances for success are significantly higher.

Wasting the First 30 Minutes

Generally, I can tell in the first 30 minutes if an investment is something that is doable for us or not. A feel for the management team, the financial condition of the company, the amount of leverage they have, their cash flow characteristics, the industry they are in—these are all things we consider. We can go through weeks of credit underwriting, but I generally know in the first half-hour if it's something we can support.

Be able to quickly articulate your business model and what problem it is solving or opportunity it is capitalizing on. This is the key. Too many times, companies are based on a technology and don't understand the market, who their customer is, or what benefit they will bring to the customer.

Missing Key Projections

Entrepreneurs' projections are seldom conservative. If they were, they would be half the size of what we typically see. I have never seen an entrepreneur achieve even his or her most conservative projections. As a rule of thumb, we typically multiply go-to-market delivery estimates and take a fraction of the revenue targets.

What are the economics? Investors are looking for means of measuring your progress, often in the form of metrics that can be measured. Many of these metrics are economic: revenue per headcount, expense per headcount, marginal gross margins, revenue per customer, cumulative units to break-even, and so forth.

Own-opinion Bias: "Our Research Indicates ..."

"A $50 billion market in five years" is simply not believable. Entrepreneurs who attempt to cater to everyone in a market often satisfy (and attract investments) from no one!

Who will buy it, and how will you sell it to them? That is, how do you segment your potential customers, and what is your plan to efficiently make them aware of your product and decide to give you money in exchange for it?

Cliché Reliance: "One Percent of the Market ..."

Very few investors are interested in a company that only wants 1 percent of any market. Instead, we'd rather see an appreciation for the difficulty of building a successful company.

How will you make money? This may be obvious for some companies ("We will sell widgets for $10 each"), but not so obvious for many others. Software, for example, can be sold on a per-user or per-site basis, with or without recurring licensing fees, with or without recurring maintenance fees, with or without installation or customization fees, and so forth. Or, you could give away the razor and make your money on blades.

Wanting the Whole Grape Instead of a Slice of the Watermelon

Surround yourself with really smart people and appropriately compensate them. It's better to have a smaller piece of a huge pie than to have an entire really small pie. There are some entrepreneurs who could bring in the founder of Amazon.com as an advisor, but they don't want to give him any equity because they want to maintain the entire thing—but that could be just the tipping point that would propel them to the next major level. Surround yourself with really, really smart people.

Tell Them Instead of Showing Them

A simple visual proof-of-concept of what you are trying to do goes a long way in terms of getting your ideas financed. *Show* them as much as you can.

Ignoring the "Dinner Table Rule"

Don't raise money from anyone you wouldn't want to have dinner with every week.

Going at It Alone

It is difficult to build your company by yourself. You need to bring in advisors to counsel and coach you as you progress—people who can support your vision but at the same time keep you on track and focused. Even the best athletes in the world have trainers and coaches, mentors, and support resources.

Relying upon Pending Executives with Funding

Often during due diligence, we found out that many "executive commitments" were actually nothing more than casual conversations. Executives with strong compensation plans in stable positions will seldom leave to join a highly risky venture. It is much more credible if you can physically bring some of the key individuals to the due-diligence table.

After You Take Their Money

Turning Down an Investor

In general, you should work your hardest not to turn an investor down. Either try to build them into the syndicate or get them involved in some way. The world is pretty small, and if someone shows that much interest in your company, you should work hard to cut them in for at least some sort of piece. When they go through that learning process with you to get to the next level, why not give that person a smaller piece in that round, with the opportunity to have a larger piece in the next? Create a situation where everyone has some sort of opportunity.

Not Knowing the "Who"

It's the "who" that gets us all in trouble. I can think of some real tragic stories. For example, a technology graduate of Georgia Tech built a terrific little company, needed additional capital, and brought in some very savvy investors. Today, they own the company and he is looking for a job. That sort of situation really shows that, in the way you structure these transactions, the integrity—who it is you are doing business with—matters. When I look at our client acceptance protocol, we are doing everything we can to evaluate who we do business with rather than the characteristics of the business, because it is the who that gets us all in trouble.

Taking the Highest Valuation

The more resources entrepreneurs have, the more informed they will be—and that is exactly what they need. One entrepreneur noted, "We picked the VC we did because we got the highest valuation from them. In hindsight, that was the wrong decision. If we had picked the VC that I work with now instead, we would have gotten a lower valuation but had a better VC, and that would have been a better decision."

Another entrepreneur stated, "From my perspective, the two most damaging mistakes made early on are not raising enough capital and trying to set a valuation too early."

"I'm always dumbfounded when people use a lot of present-value models to establish valuations," said a third. "The only valuation model that I've ever thought made sense is precedent. What are venture investors investing in that particular company at that particular time?"

Misrepresented Sense of Urgency

"Just because the investment timing was important to us, it didn't mean that it was to them. We created a false sense of urgency by name-dropping other investors who were 'interested' and it backfired, as many VC firms know each other and compare investment opportunities for syndication."

Claiming a Proven Management Team When it's Not

There are two problems with touting an inexperienced management team as "proven." First, if they were that proven, they wouldn't be in the investors' office asking for money. Second, it takes very different skills to take a company from $500 million to $2 billion than it does from zero to $5 million.

Go in with relevant experience. Convince them that you will do whatever it takes to succeed. Surround yourselves with proven and very relevant advisors. Offer to step aside whenever the business requires more than your skills or capacity/capability can execute.

Taking on the Wrong Venture Capital Firm

If you bring in the wrong VC, it can destroy your company. The most important things to understand are the gravity of bringing in different kinds of money and how your mistakes have much greater consequences once you have accepted that money. You have to be prepared for that kind of money. Have a CFO in place—a very senior financial person—who is prepared for the reporting requirements and oversight and really understands what you are getting into.

Playing Securities Lawyer

A lot of entrepreneurs have been known to "play lawyer" to save a buck. Unfortunately, play lawyers are no match for state and federal securities laws and the regulators who enforce them. For example, when it comes to raising investment capital, many entrepreneurs have heard of Regulation D securities offerings, but most have no idea that there are *three kinds* of offerings available under Regulation D, each with its own set of restrictions and nuances.

The reality is that federal and state securities laws are frequently obtuse. Even the best amateur lawyer will eventually end up in hot water by overlooking small details. Always engage the assistance of a professional when selling securities in your company. Try the referral service of your local bar association for a recommendation.

Waiting Too Long to Get the Cash in

When it is a small amount of money (under $1 million), set it up on a short time frame. Take whatever you can get at whatever price you can get—be quick and be done.

Misunderstanding Value Creation

You can build a lot of value with very little capital. That value is in terms of people, intellectual property, and the relationships you have built. Focus on those types of things at the early stage rather than doing things like product development and permits.

Staying in a Bad Marriage

At worst, the result of sticking with the wrong investor is that your business will not succeed. Your competitors catch up and overtake you, you run out of cash because previous investors are not willing to reinvest, and so on. If there is a mismatch, identify it early. Have an investor buy out a previous one. Identify the problem early and rectify it.

Hoping for a Fortune 500 Company Order

"They are going to sign our purchase order next week" telegraphs unpredictability. Investors are too savvy to accept "hope" as a strategy. Communicate confidence with only that which you can deliver.

Having too Many Lenders or Investors

One of the hazards of securing financing from multiple sources is managing too many relationships and expectations. It takes time away from your core business. These not-so-silent partners may have conflicting interests or demands, and the consequences can be devastating.

Failing to Get the Proper Legal Agreements

Proper legal documentation with investors is arguably more important than a prenuptial agreement for a couple with significant individual assets. Every lender or investor will eventually need his money back, and a legal document covering everything from the terms to the timing can avoid an acrimonious dissolution.

Poor Cash-flow Management

I'm amazed at how many new entrepreneurs burn through their seed money way too fast and fail to reach positive cash flow in a timely manner. Late product deliveries and economic downturns may be beyond one's control, but the leadership team is clearly at fault for others, such as unnecessary spending and overly optimistic profit-and-loss forecasts. Investors don't take kindly to mismanagement, and if they turn off the financing tap, all of the entrepreneur's hard work is likely to go down the drain.

Growing a Business as an Acquisition Opportunity

I don't think you can grow a company specifically to be an acquisition opportunity. I think you have to grow a company to be a stand-alone business, and if an acquisition comes along, that's great. Having said that, when you are doing deals—when you are creating the company—you should always look at every partnership and think, If I do that partnership, will it hurt the ability to do an acquisition? Or, How can I change that contract so I can still do an acquisition with a potentially competitive company?

Misunderstanding the Customer's Needs

One entrepreneur noted, "After the acquisition, our customers never really bought the products and services [from the company we acquired]. We assumed they were complementary to our own. We misjudged their needs and ended up with two completely unintegrated customer bases and product lines—a very expensive and unwieldy proposition we're still trying to address two years after the acquisition."

Overestimating Cost Savings

One entrepreneur thought that significant savings could be squeezed out of an acquired company by moving field functions such as sales, administration, and service into centralized headquarters. "What we found was that the acquired company's competitive advantage was very much the function of these field functions. Customers missed the continuity through our consolidation and we had to rebuild—and often hire back (more expensively)—the same resources we had dismantled."

Underestimating Customer Fallout

Any time you acquire another company, you are going to lose some of the other company's customers. Don't assume that sales or revenues will be the same after your acquisition as they were before it—at least, not in the short term.

Cultural Mismatches

Look at the way the acquisition target relates to its customers, suppliers, and employers. Make sure that its culture is complementary to yours.

SUMMARY

☑ A great deal of fundraising wisdom can be gained from the experience of having made bad decisions and learning in the process from other entrepreneurs who have already traveled this journey.

☑ Entrepreneurs, intermediaries, and investors alike contribute their painful lessons in the past in three time frames: before you begin the process, in the midst of your fundraising efforts, and after you accept investors' money.

☑ Successful fundraising is a moving target and one that requires lifelong learning.

Appendixes

APPENDIX A: THE ULTIMATE RESOURCE LIBRARY

During my research, I thought it would be helpful to put together a resource directory of sources other entrepreneurs and investors have referred me to. Please understand that by no means are these five hundred sources all-inclusive, nor does inclusion in this directory constitute an endorsement. I would encourage your standard level of due diligence and care in the evaluation of any of these sources. The materials in this section are copyrighted by their respective owners.

This appendix of websites to explore is categorized into general, specific industry, and a handful of regional resources. Here are the major headings—note that many sites are applicable in multiple categories:

1. How to Get Funded
2. Where to Find Angels
3. Loans and Grants
4. Venture Capital Resources
5. Business Planning and Research
6. Marketing Best Practices
7. Financial and Operational Stewardship
8. Legal Insights
9. General Science
10. Nanotechnology and Microelectromechanical Systems
11. Technology and Telecommunications
12. Arizona
13. Atlanta
14. Boston
15. Los Angeles
16. New York
17. San Diego
18. Seattle
19. San Francisco Bay Area/Silicon Valley

Besides Arizona and New York, many other states have similar resources; search Google to find one in your area. Visit www.relationshipeconomics. net/raisingcapital.html for access to the most up-to-date online directory of this information, including search capabilities, feedback from other entrepreneurs on their usefulness, and tips and techniques on how to get the most from each resource.

How to Get Funded

American Venture
http://www.americanventuremaga-zine.com/
Online edition of the publication for founders, investors, and service providers of early-stage innovative technology-based companies.

BizAZ's Entrepreneur Resource Guide
http://republicmediasolutions.com/
Listings of service providers throughout Arizona.

The Gauntlet
http://www.the-gauntlet.com/?affil=cayc
The Gauntlet is an online service that tests you and your business to see if you're ready for investment. It works like a virtual investor, challenging you to answer all of the critical questions investors will ask and explaining why they ask them. There is a modest fee for running the tests and receiving your report. Although I have not tried it out, it certainly appears worthwhile.

Go Big Network
http://www.gobignetwork.com/
The Go Big Network is an online community that connects entrepreneurs, investors, and other individuals that play a role in the start-up business world.

High-Tech Start-up Valuation Estimator

http://www.caycon.com/valuation.php
Wondering what your premoney valuation will be if a venture capitalist ever puts a term sheet on the table? Answer the questions here, and the site will calculate an approximate range for you. Of course, every situation is different, so your mileage may vary.

Reg D Resources
http://www.regdresources.com/
Don't have thousand of dollars to have a securities attorney prepare your offering documents? Regulation D Resources provides a do-it-yourself solution.

Resources for Entrepreneurs by Gaebler Ventures
http://www.gaebler.com/writing-a-business-plan.htm
A collection of short articles on business planning, capital formation, and related topics.

Tannedfeet.com
http://www.tannedfeet.com/
A large, well-organized collection of articles on entrepreneurship, marketing, legal, financial, and related issues.

TechCrunch
http://www.techcrunch.com/
TechCrunch allows you to upload a 60-second elevator pitch for your start-up and have your pitch voted on and critiqued by peers.

Venture Blog
http://www.ventureblog.com/
Read this. It'll make you a smarter
entrepreneur, guaranteed.

Where to Find Angels

Active Capital
http://activecapital.org/index.html
Formerly known as Angel Capital
Electronic Network (ACE-Net),
Active Capital is a matchmaking
service for accredited investors and
entrepreneurs. It also provides
resources for entrepreneurs, such as
information on how to properly
comply with regulations.

Alliance of Angels
http://www.allianceofangels.com/
Angel investor group in the Seattle
region.

Angel Blog
http://www.angelblog.net/
Angel Blog is a forum for experienced
entrepreneurs and successful angel
investors to develop and share ideas
on how to improve their skills and
tools for rapidly growing, successful
tech companies.

Angel Capital Association's *Directory
of Angel Organizations*
http://www.angelcapitalassociation.
org/dir_directory/directory.aspx
Directory of 200 angel investor groups
throughout North America.

Angel Investor Directory
http://www.inc.com/articles/2001/
09/23461.html
A directory of angel investor groups
organized by region, including
descriptions of the types of ventures
they are interested in, typical investment amounts, and contact
information.

Angel Investor News
http://www.angel-investor-news.
com/
News, articles, and resources for
entrepreneurs and angel investors.

AngelDeals.com
http://www.angeldeals.com/
Connects entrepreneurs, investors,
opportunities, and resources.

AngelSearch
http://www.vfinance.com/
Fee-based search by location, net worth,
investment interests, and more.

Atlanta Technology Angels
http://www.angelatlanta.com/
Angel investor group in the Atlanta
region.

Band of Angels
http://www.bandangels.com/
Angel investor group in the Silicon
Valley region.

Gathering of Angels
http://www.gatheringofangels.com/
This group organizes monthly presentations for entrepreneurs in selected
cities.

Investors' Circle
http://www.investorscircle.net/
Investors' Circle is an angel network
consisting of more than 200 angel
investors, professional venture capitalists, foundations, family offices,
and others dedicated to promoting
entrepreneurs who have ventures in
sustainability or social and environmental responsibility.

New Mexico Private Investors
http://www.nmangels.com/
Angel investment group based in
Albuquerque, New Mexico.

Pasadena Angels
http://www.pasadenaangels.com/
Angel investor group in Pasadena,
 California.

Tech Coast Angels
http://www.techcoastangels.com/
Angel investor group in Southern
 California.

Tribe of Angels/Jewish Business
 Network
http://www.tribeofangels.com/
Tribe of Angels is an angel organization designed to address the needs
 of Jewish investors, entrepreneurs,
 and executives. The networking
 group has more than 5,000 members
 and has operations in Boston, California, Chicago, Connecticut, New
 York, and Israel.

Vegas Valley Angels
http://www.vegasvalleyangels.com/
Angel investing group in southern
 Nevada.

Winter Park Angels
http://www.winterparkangels.com/
Angel group located in central
 Florida.

Loans and Grants

Community of Science
http://www.cos.com/
Community of Science is the leading
 Internet site for the global R&D
 community, including a directory of
 more than 400,000 funding
 opportunities.

Defense Advanced Research Projects
 Agency (DARPA)
http://www.darpa.mil/
Funding for technologies with potential military applications.

Department of Defense
http://www.acq.osd.mil/osbp/sbir/
Department of Defense Small Business
 Innovation Research and Small Business Technology Transfer programs.

Environmental Protection Agency (EPA)
http://www.epa.gov/ogd/recipient/
 tips.htm
Grant-writing tips from EPA.

Foundation Center
http://foundationcenter.org/
Helping grant seekers succeed, and
 helping grant makers make a
 difference.

GrantsNet
http://sciencecareers.sciencemag.org/
GrantsNet is a directory of funding
 sources for training in the biomedical sciences.

National Association of Development
 Companies (NADCO)
http://www.nadco.org/
Companies certified by the Small
 Business Administration (SBA) to
 provide funding to small businesses
 under the SBA 504 loan program.

National Institutes of Health (NIH)
http://grants1.nih.gov/grants/oer.htm
Grants and funding opportunities
 focused on health sciences. NIH
 grant-writing tips sheets are available at http://grants1.nih.gov/
 grants/grant_tips.htm.

National Science Foundation (NSF)
http://www.nsf.gov/funding/
Listing of NSF funding opportunities.
 The *NSF Guide for Proposal Writing* is
 available at http://www.nsf.gov/
 pubs/1998/nsf9891/nsf9891.htm.

Small Business Administration (SBA)
http://www.sba.gov/aboutsba/sbap-
rograms/sbir/index.html
Funding for technological innovation
through the Small Business Innovation Research (SBIR) and Small Business Technology Transfer (STTR)
programs.

Securities and Exchange Commission
(SEC)
http://www.sec.gov/info/smallbus/
qasbsec.htm
A guide to help you understand how
to raise capital and comply with federal securities laws.

Technology Grant News
http://www.technologygrantnews.
com/
Covers the up-and-coming grant
announcements by government
agencies, technology funders,
trade associations, and private-
sector foundations around the
country.

Venture Capital Resources

BusinessFinance.com
http://www.businessfinance.com/
A directory of over 78,000 business
loan and venture capital sources.

CapitalHunter.com
http://www.capitalhunter.com/
A financial information company that
identifies and disseminates national
data on venture capital and other
equity financings.

DealBook
http://dealbook.blogs.nytimes.com/
category/venture-capital/
A roundup of recent venture capital-
related news from the *New York
Times.*

Funding Universe
http://www.fundinguniverse.com/

One of the better online forums for
matching angel investors and
entrepreneurs.

Google's Venture Capital Directory
http://directory.google.com/Top/
Business/Financial_Services/
Venture_Capital/

Growthink Venture Capital Research
http://www.growthinkresearch.com/
Growthink Research publishes venture capital funding and private
equity reports that analyze financing
trends for emerging companies. In
addition to publishing dozens of
"off-the-shelf" funding research
reports, Growthink also performs cli-
ent-specific market and competitive
research projects.

National Venture Capital Association
http://www.nvca.org/

PricewaterhouseCoopers/Venture
Economics MoneyTree Survey
https://www.pwcmoneytree.com/
The MoneyTree Survey is a quarterly
study of venture capital investment
activity in the United States. As a
collaboration between PricewaterhouseCoopers, Thomson Venture
Economics, and the National Venture
Capital Association, it is the only
industry-endorsed research of its kind.

VC Experts
http://vcexperts.com/vce/
VC Experts serves the needs of the
private equity and venture capital
communities with its anchor
product, the 4,000-page *The Encyclopedia of Private Equity and Venture
Capital*, by combining substantive
commentary on the private equity
and venture capital industries with
online learning courses. The Web
site includes current industry news,
weekly commentary, the online
university, and the encyclopedia.

VC Fodder
http://www.vcfodder.com/
No-nonsense tips and advice for
  entrepreneurs.

Venture Blog
http://www.ventureblog.com/
A must-read for astute entrepreneurs!

Venture One
http://www.ventureone.com/
Venture One offers investors, service
  providers, and entrepreneurs the
  most comprehensive, accurate, and
  timely information on the venture
  capital industry.

Venture Reporter
https://www.fis.dowjones.com/
Venture capital deals, news, articles,
  and more.

Venture Wire
http://www.fis.dowjones.com/prod-
  ucts/vc.html
Sign up for the free e-mail updates of
  the deals that are getting funded.

vFinance.com
http://www.vfinance.com/ent/ent.
  asp?Toolpage=vencaentire.asp
A directory of more than 1,600 venture capital firms (scroll down the
  linked page to see the list).

Business Planning and Research

10kWizard
http://www.10kwizard.com/
Access SEC filings, company financials, and so forth.

About.com: Entrepreneurship
http://entrepreneurs.about.com/

Extensive, well-organized, and frequently updated directory of articles
  and resources for entrepreneurs.

AllBusiness.com
http://www.allbusiness.com/
An expansive, well-organized collection of entrepreneurial resources and
  advice, including business forums,
  news, and blogs aimed at smaller
  businesses.

Always On
http://alwayson.goingon.com/
Traditional news and analysis, blog-
  ging, and a social network for senior
  executives, technologists, and investors from a broad selection of
  industries.

American Heritage Dictionary
http://www.bartleby.com/61/

Answers.com
http://www.answers.com/
General reference resource—kind of a
  hybrid encyclopedia, almanac,
  dictionary, and thesaurus, among
  other things.

Bancroft Information Services
http://www.bancroftinfo.com/
Bancroft Information Services provides customized business intelligence and "secondary" market
  research to support business plans,
  marketing strategies, and new business development for high-tech
  start-ups, marketing strategists,
  advertising agencies, software
  firms, publishers, authors, sales
  consultants, corporate trainers,
  and others.

Better Business Bureau
http://www.bbbonline.org/
Know whom you're doing business
  with.

BizzBangBuzz
http://bizzbangbuzz.blogspot.com/
The entrepreneur law blog of Pitts-
  burgh strategic business and technology attorney Anthony Cerminaro,
  focused on small business, venture
  capital, entrepreneurship, technology, and other items of interest to
  entrepreneurs.

Bloomberg
http://www.bloomberg.com/
Good source of financial data.

Bplans.com
http://www.bplans.com/
Business plan preparation software
  and sample business plans. Also
  includes tips for writing business
  plans.

Business Filings
http://www.bizfilings.com/
Incorporation information and online
  corporate formation.

Business Owner's Idea Café
http://www.businessownersideacafe.
  com/
A large collection of resources for
  entrepreneurs.

Business Owner's Toolkit
http://www.toolkit.com/
Complete knowledge base for small
  business.

Business Plan Archive
http://www.businessplanarchive.org/
An archive of business plans and
  other materials used by real
  start-ups.

Businesstown
http://www.businesstown.com/
  default.asp
An extensive, well-organized directory of resources for entrepreneurs.

Center for Business Planning
http://www.businessplans.org/
Business plan software, samples
  (includes the winning business plans
  from the Moot Corp business plan
  competition), and strategy.

CEO Express
http://www.ceoexpress.com/
Digest and links to just about everything a CEO would need to read.

Club E Network
http://www.clubenetwork.com/
Club E is an online and offline network where entrepreneurs can meet
  peers, get feedback, and exchange
  ideas. The Web site also offers video
  content for entrepreneurs, as well as
  tools for exchange of services.

Columbia Encyclopedia
http://www.bartleby.com/65/
The Company Corporation
http://www.incorporate.com/
Incorporate online, including name
  searches, tax ID applications, compliance services, and more.

Competitive Intelligence Directory
http://www.fuld.com/TIndex/I3.html
An extensive directory compiled by
  Fuld & Co.

Corporate Information
http://www.corporateinformation.
  com/
Access to extensive and insightful collection of corporate research.

CorpTech Technology Company Information
http://www.corptech.com/
CorpTech publishes public and private business information on technology companies that make, develop, and provide services related to everything from lasers to computers, and from biotech products to advanced materials.

DataMonitor
http://www.datamonitor.com/
Background information on numerous industries.

Delaware Corporate Information
https://sos-res.state.de.us/tin/GINameSearch.jsp
Look up exact legal names, dates of incorporation, and related information.

The Economist
http://www.economist.com/
In-depth reporting and analysis of the international economy and the events and developments that affect it.

Economy.com
http://www.economy.com/default.asp
A great deal of economic data and research available at the metro, state, and country levels, as well as by industry.

Edward Lowe Foundation
http://edwardlowe.org/
Plenty of excellent entrepreneurial resources.

eMarketer
http://www.emarketer.com/
E-business, Internet, and technology market data and analysis aggregated from numerous sources.

Entrepreneur.com
http://www.entrepreneur.com/interstitial/default.html
Entrepreneurial resources.

Entrepreneur Meetup
http://entrepreneur.meetup.com/
Meet a network of local entrepreneurs to share tips and problem-solving techniques, get advice on profitability and careers, and discuss mentoring and business models.

The Entrepreneur's Mind
http://www.benlore.com/
Interesting case studies we can all learn from.

Entrepreneurship at Harvard Business School
http://www.hbs.edu/entrepreneurship/
Great articles, events, and research for entrepreneurs.

EntreWorld.org
http://eventuring.kauffman.org/
An extensive directory of entrepreneurial resources.

FastCompany
http://www.fastcompany.com/
The definitive go-to source for entrepreneurs.

Fedworld
http://www.fedworld.gov/
Locate government information.

Financial Times
http://www.ft.com/
Breaking business news from an international perspective.

Food and Drug Administration (FDA)
http://www.fda.gov/cder/handbook/index.htm

Information on new drug development in the *Center for Drug Evaluation and Research (CDER) Handbook.*

Forrester Research
http://www.forrester.com/rb/
research
Covers many industries.

Fortune Small Business
http://money.cnn.com/
smallbusiness/
Entrepreneurial resources, including
frequently updated original content.

Free Edgar
http://freeedgar.com/
Access SEC filings for public companies (a limited number of free
queries per month are available,
after which you can use Yahoo
Finance).

Frost & Sullivan
http://www.frost.com/prod/servlet/
frost-home.pag
Covers many industries.

F✳✳✳ed Company
http://www.fuckedcompany.com/
Highly entertaining, but for mature
audiences; lists impending layoffs,
bankruptcies, and other bad news.
Gartner Group
http://www.gartner.com/
Covers many industries.

The Gauntlet
http://www.the-gauntlet.com/
?affil=cayc
The Gauntlet is an online service that
tests you and your business to see if
you're ready for investment. It
works like a virtual investor, challenging you to answer all of the critical questions investors will ask and
explaining why they ask them. There
is a modest fee for running the tests

and receiving your report. Although
I have not tried it out, it certainly
appears worthwhile.

GlobalEDGE
http://globaledge.msu.edu/
GlobalEDGE is a knowledge Web
portal that connects international
business professionals worldwide to
a wealth of information, insights,
and learning resources on global
business activities.

Gomez Research
http://www.gomez.com/
Emphasis on the Internet.

Growth Company Guide
http://www.growco.com/
Entrepreneurial resources, including
the complete text of the *Growth
Company Guide.*

IDC
http://www.idc.com/
Broad-based industry analysts.

Inc.
http://www.inc.com/
A must-read for entrepreneurs—an
excellent source of information on
business formation and managing
growth.
The Industry Standard
http://www.thestandard.com/
Another must-read for entrepreneurs.

Information Please
http://www.infoplease.com/
An extensive general research
resource.

Internet Public Library
http://www.ipl.org/
An extensive general research
resource.

Internet World
http://www.internetworld.com/
Internet business news, papers, and
 blogs, drawing content from sites
 like CNET and *Information Week*.

Jupiter Research
http://www.jupiterresearch.com/
Broad-based industry analysts.

Krislyn's Strictly Business Sites
http://www.strictlybusinesssites.com/
A large directory of business
 resources.

Marketing Research Association
http://www.mra-net.org/
A great deal of resources for market
 researchers.

MarketResearch.com
http://www.marketresearch.com/
Search for and buy research reports
 from all the leading market research
 companies.

MedTech Insight
http://www.medtechinsight.com/
Covers most life science fields.

MIT Enterprise Forum
http://enterpriseforum.mit.edu/
 mindshare/planning/
Business plan resources.

MIT Technology Review
http://www.technologyreview.com/

MoreBusiness.com
http://www.morebusiness.com/
Lots of great articles, tips, templates,
 and other resources.

MyWorkTools.com
http://www.myworktools.com/
A large collection of business tools in
 all areas, from legal and finance to
 marketing and business development.

NanoBusiness Alliance
http://nanoenergysummit.org/
The NanoBusiness Alliance's mission
 is to create a collective voice for the
 emerging small-tech industry and
 develop a range of initiatives to support and strengthen the nanotechnology business community. Key
 initiatives include research and education; public policy; public relations;
 international cooperation activities,
 trade missions, and events; industry
 support and development initiatives;
 and the Regional Hub Initiative.

National Association for the Self-
 Employed
http://www.nase.org/
All kinds of benefits for the self-
 employed. An essential resource if
 you're going solo; if you expect to have
 employees, check out a Professional
 Employer Organization (PEO), a service
 provider of outsourced human resource
 management, as an alternative.

National Association of Development
 Companies (NADCO)
http://www.nadco.org/
Companies certified by the SBA to
 provide funding to small businesses
 under the SBA 504 loan program.

National Business Incubator
 Association
http://www.nbia.org/
Learn about incubators and how to
 get into one most relevant to your
 focus.

National Institutes of Health
http://www.nih.gov/

NEBS Business Plan Tool
http://www.nebs.com/nebsEcat/
 business_tools/bptemplate/index.jsp
An interactive business plan writing
 resource.

New York Times Business and Technology sections
http://www.nytimes.com/pages/business/index.html
http://www.nytimes.com/pages/technology/index.html
Classic *New York Times* coverage of business and technology-related matters.

Nielsen Netratings
http://www.nielsen-netratings.com/
Emphasis on the Internet, including frequently updated usage statistics.

PartnerUp
http://www.partnerup.com/
This site allows entrepreneurs to find business partners, executives, or other personnel. In addition, users can exchange advice, find commercial real estate, and find professional service providers.

PeopleThatClick
http://www.peoplethatclick.com/home.asp
Get a free analysis of your strengths and weaknesses as an entrepreneur and find business partners who complement you in your quest to develop and grow your venture.

PlanWare
http://www.planware.org/
Software and other resources for writing business plans and financial projections.

PowerReporting.com
http://www.powerreporting.com/
Thousands of free research tools.

Red Herring
http://www.redherring.com/
The business of technology—a must-read for entrepreneurs.

Refdesk
http://www.refdesk.com/
A vast collection of reference materials.

Researching Companies Online
http://www.learnwebskills.com/company/
A helpful guide, with links to additional resources.

Roget's II: The New Thesaurus
http://www.bartleby.com/62/
Containing 35,000 synonyms and more than 250,000 cross-references in an easy-to-use format, this thesaurus features succinct word definitions and an innovative hyperlinked category index.

San Francisco Chronicle
http://www.sfgate.com/chronicle/

San Jose Mercury News
http://www.mercurynews.com/

Securities and Exchange Commission (SEC)
http://www.sec.gov/info/smallbus/qasbsec.htm
A guide to help you understand how to raise capital and comply with federal securities laws.

Service Corps of Retired Executives (SCORE)
http://www.score.org/index.html
Nonprofit association dedicated to encouraging the formation, growth, and success of small business nationwide through counseling and mentor programs.

SiliconValley.com
http://www.siliconvalley.com/

Small Business Administration (SBA)
http://www.sba.gov/

All kinds of resources for start-ups and small businesses with a wide array of free educational materials for the entrepreneur. The SBA Business Plan Outline, available at http://www.sba.gov/smallbusiness planner/index.html, includes tips on how to complete various sections of the business plan. SBA online courses can be accessed at http://www.sba.gov/services/training/index.html.

Small Business Indicators
http://www.sba.gov/advo/research/sbei.html
Small Business Indicators reports bring together monthly and quarterly data from a wide variety of sources. Entrepreneurs can use the information-packed two-page reports to learn more about what is driving the small business economy in the United States. Each quarterly report covers trends affecting small business, economic indicators over the last five years and the last five quarters, and macroeconomic statistics.

Small Business Plan Guide
http://www.smallbusinessplanguide.com/web/index.php
A comprehensive directory of business planning resources.

Social Science Data on the Net
http://ssdc.ucsd.edu/index.html
A variety of social science, government, and geographic data.

Stanford Business
http://www.gsb.stanford.edu/news/bmag/
Articles and research papers on a wide range of topics produced by the faculty of the Stanford Graduate School of Business.

Stanford Technology Ventures Program Entrepreneurial Resources
http://ecorner.stanford.edu/
An outstanding collection of entrepreneurial education resources, including video clips (of such thought leaders as John Doerr of Kliener Perkins and Guy Kawasaki, author of *The Art of Start*), podcasts, and presentations.

Startup Journal
http://online.wsj.com/small-business
The *Wall Street Journal*'s entrepreneur resource center, including frequently updated original content.

StartupBiz.com
http://www.startupbiz.com/
Entrepreneurial resources.

Stat-USA
http://www.stat-usa.gov/
Business, trade, and economic information.

Tannedfeet.com
http://www.tannedfeet.com/
A large, well-organized collection of articles on entrepreneurship, marketing, legal, financial, and related issues.

TechCrunch
http://www.techcrunch.com/
TechCrunch allows you to upload a 60-second elevator pitch for your startup and have your pitch voted on and critiqued by peers.

Teneric Professional Business Plans
http://www.teneric.co.uk/
Easily write your business or marketing plan using Teneric's expert guides. The site has a great deal of free advice, templates, and samples to download.

TheInfoPro (TIP)
http://www.theinfopro.net/

TIP is an independent research network and leading supplier of market intelligence for the information technology industry. Created by alumni of Gartner, EMC, Giga, and Bell Labs, TIP produces fundamental, objective, and analyst-free research on markets, vendors, issues, future adoption plans, and investor confidence.

U.S. Bureau of Labor Statistics
http://www.bls.gov/

U.S. Census Bureau
http://www.census.gov/

US Commercial Service
http://trade.gov/cs/
Assistance to help your business export goods and services to markets worldwide.

U.S. Department of Commerce Technology Administration
http://www.technology.gov/
The only federal agency working to maximize technology's contribution to America's economic growth.

U.S. Department of Health and Human Services
http://www.os.dhhs.gov/

U.S. Environmental Protection Agency
http://www.epa.gov/

U.S. Patent and Trademark Office
http://www.uspto.gov/
Search for granted U.S. patents and federal trademarks; learn about and apply for intellectual property (IP) protection.

Vator.tv
http://www.vator.tv/

Vator is an emerging company social network that allows entrepreneurs to connect with investors and get discovered by the media. It also provides entrepreneurial news and competitions.

Wall Street Journal
http://online.wsj.com/public/us
Most resources require a paid subscription.

Wired
http://www.wired.com/

The World Factbook
http://www.bartleby.com/151/
The U.S. government's complete geographical handbook, featuring 267 full-color maps and flags of all nations and geographical entities. Each country profile tracks such demographics as population, ethnicity, and literacy rates, as well as political, geographical, and economic data.

World Health Organization
http://www.who.int/en/

Yahoo! Finance
http://finance.yahoo.com/
An excellent source of financial information, including a link to Edgar SEC filings.

Yankee Group
http://www.yankeegroup.com/
Industry analysts in a number of industries.

ZeroMillion.com
http://www.zeromillion.com/entrepreneurship/
A wide selection of articles and other entrepreneur resources.

Marketing Best Practices

About.com
http://websearch.about.com/
Links to search engine optimization
  (SEO) resources.

American Heritage Dictionary
http://www.bartleby.com/61/

Bruce Clay, LLC
http://www.bruceclay.com/
Tons of free tips and tools for search
  engine optimization.

Business Town
http://www.businesstown.com/
  marketing/plans.asp
Marketing plans and other business
  topics.

Chicago Manual of Style
http://www.chicagomanualofstyle.
  org/home.html
An essential resource for writers.

Communitelligence.com
http://www.communitelligence.com/
Communitelligence.com is a member
  knowledge-sharing portal aimed at
  improving organizational and inter-
  personal communication, with thirty
  expert-led communities on key
  topics such as public relations, internal communication, marketing,
  presentation skills, writing, and business strategy.

DotFactor.com
http://www.dotfactor.com/
Tools, ideas, and Internet marketing
  solutions for online businesses.

Emerging Tech PR
http://www.emergingtechpr.com/
Easy-to-understand information on
  public relations for emerging tech
  companies.

English Usage, Style, and
  Composition
http://www.bartleby.com/usage/
Search across multiple resources at
  once.

GoRank
http://www.gorank.com/
Professional SEO tools for tracking
  rankings, analyzing keyword
  density, link popularity, and much
  more.

Grammar, Usage, and Style Resources
http://www.refdesk.com/factgram.
  html

Internet Marketing Tools
http://www.biznetcenter.com/
Features a comparison of Internet
  marketing products, eBooks, training
  videos, software, and services.

KnowThis.com
http://www.knowthis.com/
Knowledge source for market
  research, marketing plans, Internet
  marketing, marketing careers, and
  much more.

MarcommWise
http://www.marcommwise.com/
Marketing communications articles,
  book reviews, glossary, and other
  related resources.
Free, Java-based calculators are available at http://www.marcommwise.
  com/calcindex.phtml for estimating
  the profitability of clicks-and impres-
  sion-based Web advertising and
  direct mail campaigns, as well as the
  lifetime value of customers.

Marketing Power
http://www.marketingpower.com/
  Pages/default.aspx
A marketing portal created by the
  American Marketing Association.

Marketing Showroom
http://www.marketingshowroom.com/
A collection of Web-based marketing items that can help grow and market your business, chosen by marketing professionals based on personal experiences and client needs.

Marketing Today
http://www.marketingtoday.com/
The online guide to marketing in the Information Age.

MarketingProfs.com
http://www.marketingprofs.com/
Marketing know-how from professors and professionals.

The Mother of All Marketing for Business Owners
http://motherofallmarketing.com/
An e-book on advertising and marketing strategies and tactics for consumer-facing retail business owners.

Mplans.com
http://www.mplans.com/dpm/
Marketing plan software and sample marketing plans.

Overture's Search Term Suggestion Tool
http://sem.smallbusiness.yahoo.com/searchenginemarketing/
Enter a keyword or phrase to see how frequently people search on that and similar terms. Very useful for deciding on title, header, and meta keyword tags.

Pay Per Click Search Engines
http://www.payperclicksearchengines.com/
A good guide to how pay-per-click search engines work.

PR Web
http://www.prweb.com/

Affordable online press release distribution.

Professional Writing Handouts and Resources
http://owl.english.purdue.edu/owl/resource/681/01/
This collection of articles covers many important aspects of business, technical, and professional writing.

ROI Calculator
http://www.pageviews.com/resources/roicalculator/resources2.php
Use this calculator to determine the return on investment (ROI) of a search engine marketing campaign.

Search Engine Guide
http://www.searchengineguide.com/
Lots of resources related to search engines and SEO.

Search Engine Marketing
http://www.clickz.com/
This is the ClickZ (formerly Internet-Day) site that carries articles on search engine marketing.

Search Engine Ranking and Keyword Tracker
http://www.digitalpoint.com/tools/keywords/
Free tool for tracking the performance of various keywords on multiple search engines.

Search Engine Relationship Chart
http://www.bruceclay.com/searchenginerelationshipchart.htm
Interactive Flash-based chart showing which search engines and directories power which others. Click on any engine to see details about it.

Search Engine Watch
http://searchenginewatch.com/

Search Engine World
http://www.searchengineworld.com/
An excellent source for learning about
 SEO and site promotion.

SearchEngineChannel
http://www.searchenginechannel.com/
SEO articles submitted by contributing
 authors from that industry.

SelfPromotion.com
http://selfpromotion.com/
Straightforward overview of SEO,
 along with some nifty free tools.

SEOpros
http://www.seopros.org/
A nonprofit organization of SEO professionals with very good tools for
 identifying and retaining a capable
 SEO consultant.

Software Pricing Resource
http://www.softwarepricing.com/
A resource for companies facing pricing decisions or who feel their pricing or discounting practices are "not
 quite right."

Website Grader
http://www.websitegrader.com/
An SEO tool that measures the marketing effectiveness of a Web site.

Writing That Works
http://www.writingthatworks.com/
Original articles and resources for
 professional business
 communications.

Financial and Operational Stewardship

Benefits Link
http://benefitslink.com/index.html
Compliance information and tools for
 employee benefit plan sponsors,
 service providers, and participants.

Business Ethics
http://www.businessethics.ca/
Features articles and other resources
 related to business ethics, corporate
 social responsibility, and the like.

Business Know-How
http://www.businessknowhow.com/
Succeed in your small business, home
 business, or career with help from
 Business Know-How.

CFO.com
http://www.cfo.com/
Lots of resources, news, and information for financial management.

Craigslist
http://www.craigslist.org/about/
 sites.html
Recruiting and other resources.

Dice.com
http://www.dice.com/
Recruiting for technical talent.

Entrepreneur.com
http://www.entrepreneur.com/
Lists insurance sources (http://www.
 entrepreneur.com/insurance/index.
 html) and small business tax centers
 (http://www.entrepreneur.com/
 tax/index.html).

Entrepreneur's Library
http://www.caycon.com/resources.php
Numerous articles and tips for business insurance.

ERI Economic Research Institute
http://www.erieri.com/
Free compensation analyst resources.

Executive Employment Agreements
http://www.executiveemployment
 agreements.com/

Information on negotiating and structuring executive employment agreements, including checklists and examples.

HomeBusinessResearch.com
http://www.homebusinessresearch.
  com/

Hotjobs.com
http://hotjobs.yahoo.com/
Recruiting for all positions.

Human Resources Outsourcing Kit
http://www.hr-outsourcing.org/
Human resources (HR) outsourcing materials, including service-level agreements, outsourcing contracts, transition plans, and HR audit tools.

Internal Revenue Service (IRS)
http://www.irs.gov/

LoopNet
http://www.loopnet.com/
Commercial real estate listings around the country.

Monster.com
http://www.monster.com/
Recruiting for all positions.

MyWorkTools.com
http://www.myworktools.com/
A large collection of business tools in all areas, from legal and finance to marketing and business development.

National Association for the Self-Employed
http://www.nase.org/
All kinds of benefits for the self-employed. An essential resource if you're going solo; if you expect to have employees, check out a Professional Employer Organization (PEO), a service provider of outsourced

human resource management, as an alternative.

Occupational Safety and Health Administration (OSHA)
http://www.osha.gov/
Employee safety guidelines and regulations.

Offices2Share.com
http://www.offices2share.com/
Short-term space solutions.

PaycheckCity.com
http://www.paycheckcity.com/
Online collection of paycheck calculators, ideal for what-if payroll calculations and off-cycle payroll checks.

Paychex.com
http://www.paychex.com/
A typical payroll and benefits outsourcing company.

PeopleThatClick
http://www.peoplethatclick.com/
Get a free analysis of your strengths and weaknesses as an entrepreneur, and find business partners who complement you in your quest to develop and grow your venture.

Small Business Administration (SBA) Online Courses
http://www.sba.gov/services/
  training/index.html
A wide array of free educational materials for the entrepreneur.

Small Business Taxes and Management
http://www.smbiz.com/
Tax information and strategy, updated daily.

Snap Hire
http://www.snaphire.com/

An award-winning suite of recruitment and retention tools that can help optimize and grow your networks of talent and talent sources.

Solo Entrepreneur
http://www.solo-e.com/
Information and resources for the solo entrepreneur.

Startup Zone
http://www.startupzone.com/
Startup Zone is an online recruitment site dedicated to high-growth pre-IPO start-ups.

Tax and Accounting Sites Directory
http://www.taxsites.com/

Legal Insights

AllBusiness Legal Forms
http://www.allbusiness.com/
3470951-1.html
Purchase legal form templates for corporate matters.

Business Filings
http://www.bizfilings.com/
Incorporation information and online corporate formation.

The Company Corporation
http://www.incorporate.com/
Incorporate online, including name searches, tax ID applications, compliance services, and more.

Delphion
http://www.delphion.com/
Intellectual property (IP) research and tools, including prior art searches and searches of international patent databases.

esp@cenet
http://ep.espacenet.com/
Search European patent databases.

European Patent Office
http://www.epo.org/
Information about European patents.

FindLaw
http://www.findlaw.com/
The Yahoo! of law, covering virtually any aspect of law you might care about. Includes a directory of attorneys by location and specialty.

FindLaw Contracts
http://contracts.corporate.findlaw.
com/type/index.html
Actual legal contracts used by technology companies.

FreePatentsOnline.com
http://www.freepatentsonline.com/
Searchable database of U.S. patents, from which entire patents can be downloaded in .pdf versions.

Intellectual Property Law
http://www.intelproplaw.com/
Covers IP, patent, trademark, and trademark law.

Japanese Patent Office
http://www.jpo.go.jp/
Basic information about the Japanese Patent Office. To search patents, scroll down and select "Searching IPDL (Industrial Property Digital Library)," and then select "Searching PAJ" in the second paragraph.

LegalForms.com
http://www.legalforms.com/

NOLO
http://www.nolo.com/
Extensive legal self-help resources, covering both corporate and personal law; includes forms, a legal encyclopedia and dictionary, case law, state and federal codes, and more.

Patent Cooperation Treaty (PCT)
Resources
http://www.uspto.gov/web/offices/
pac/dapps/pct/
Basic information about international
IP protection.

Patent Law
http://law.cornell.edu/

Patent Retrieval
http://www.pat2pdf.org/

Trademark Reference
http://www.cscprotectsbrands.com/
Trademark information and tools,
including a free basic search, as
well as more powerful fee-based
services.

U.S. Copyright Office
http://www.copyright.gov/
Extensive information on copyright
protections.

U.S. Patent and Trademark Office
http://www.uspto.gov/
Search for granted U.S. patents and
federal trademarks, or learn about
and apply for IP protection.

World Intellectual Property
Organization
http://www.wipo.int/portal/index.
html.en
Comprehensive information on international IP protection

General Science

AgBio Forum
http://www.agbioforum.org/
A journal devoted to the economics
and management of
agrobiotechnology.

American Heart Association
http://www.americanheart.org/

A large collection of resources related
to cardiovascular conditions and
treatments.

American Medical Association
http://www.ama-assn.org/
Extensive resources related to health
policy, advocacy, ethics, and
related subjects for health care
professionals.

Aunt Minnie
http://www.auntminnie.com/
Interventional radiology resources.

BioDevicesBiz
http://www.biodevicesbiz.com/
Portal and business-to-business marketplace sponsored by CanBiotech.

Bio-Link.org
http://www.bio-link.org/
Educating the biotechnology
workforce.

BioPharma
http://www.biopharma.com/
Biopharmaceutical products in the
U.S. market.

Bioportfolio
http://www.bioportfolio.com/
A portal for the biotech industry.

Bioresearch Online
http://www.bioresearchonline.com/
Buy and sell biotech products and
services.

BioSpace
http://www.biospace.com/
Web solutions for the life sciences,
including a portal and search
services.

Biotech and Genomics
http://news.yahoo.com/fc/science/
biotechnology_and_genetics

BioTech Reference Tools
http://biotech.icmb.utexas.edu/

Biotechnology Industry Organization
http://www.bio.org/

Biotechnology Information Directory
http://biotech.cato.com/
More than 1,500 URLs of companies,
  research institutes, universities, sources of information, and other directories specific to biotechnology,
  pharmaceutical development, and
  related fields.

Biotechnology Institute
http://www.biotechinstitute.org/
A national nonprofit organization
  dedicated to education and research
  about the present and future impact
  of biotechnology.

CanBiotech
http://www.canbiotech.com/
BioPharma portal and business-to-
  business marketplace.

Circulation
http://circ.ahajournals.org/
One of the American Heart Association's journals.

Commission on Professionals in Science and Technology
http://www.cpst.org/
The commission is charged with collecting, analyzing, and disseminating
  reliable information about the
  human resources of the United
  States in the fields of science and
  technology; promoting the best possible programs of education and
  training for potential scientists, engineers, and technicians; and developing policies for the utilization of
  scientific and technological human
  resources by educational institutions,

industry, and government for the
optimum benefit to the nation.

Community of Science
http://www.cos.com/
Community of Science is the leading
Internet site for the global R&D
community, including a directory of
more than 400,000 funding
opportunities.

Council for Biotechnology Information
http://www.whybiotech.com/
An industry organization designed to
  improve understanding and acceptance of biotechnology by collecting
  balanced, credible, and science-based
  information.

DNA Microarrays Resource
http://www.dnamicroarrays.info/
Introduction to microarray technology, links to DNA microarray software, microarray protocols,
  literature, and microarray groups
  and labs.

EurekAlert!
http://www.eurekalert.org/
A directory of science news organized
  by subject, sponsored by the American Association for the Advancement of Science.

Food and Drug Administration (FDA)
http://www.fda.gov/
Information on new drug development is available in the *Center for
  Drug Evaluation and Research (CDER)
  Handbook* (http://www.fda.gov/
  cder/handbook/index.htm).

Genetic Engineering News
http://www.genengnews.com/
The most widely read publication in
  the biotechnology field worldwide.

Gray's Anatomy
http://www.bartleby.com/107/

No, not the television show—the classic reference on human anatomy.

Health Industry Distributors Association
http://www.hida.org/

IBM Research
http://www.research.ibm.com/

Informagen
http://www.informagen.com/index.html
Software-as-a-service (SaaS) provider of bioinfomatics tools, biotechnology databases, and consulting services to the genomics, proteomics, and biopharmaceutical industries.

MedDev Group (MDG)
http://www.meddevgroup.org/
MDG is a medical device and technology networking organization whose purpose is to enhance business development opportunities for its members. Forum meetings occur monthly, usually on the first Wednesday of each month.

Medem's Medical Library
http://www.medem.com/medlb/medlib_entry.cfm
A comprehensive directory of diseases, conditions, therapies, and health strategies.

Medical Devicelink
http://www.devicelink.com/

MIT Science Library
http://libraries.mit.edu/science/
Links to a wide variety of scientific resources.

National Institutes of Health
http://www.nih.gov/
A directory of all NIH-affiliated institutes, centers, and offices can be found at http://www.nih.gov/icd/.

Nature
http://www.nature.com/index.html
Extensive, in-depth content covering topics such as biotechnology, the brain, cells and molecules, chemistry, Earth, the environment, health and medicine, physics, policy, space, and technology.

New York Times Science section
http://www.nytimes.com/pages/science/index.html

NewScientist
http://www.newscientist.com/news.ns
General science news.

Oak Ridge National Laboratory Review
http://www.ornl.gov/info/ornlreview/
Highlights current R&D activities.

OneScience.com
http://www.onescience.com/
As a resource for pharmaceutical and biotechnology jobs, OneScience offers career insight and news for the biotechnology, pharmaceutical, and medical device industries.

Online Medical Dictionary
http://cancerweb.ncl.ac.uk/omd/index.html
An extensive online medical dictionary.

Pharmaceutical Research and Manufacturers of America
http://www.phrma.org/

PhysLink
http://www.physlink.com/Reference/Index.cfm
Physics and astronomy reference resources.

Protein Data Bank
http://www.rcsb.org/pdb/home/home.do

The single worldwide repository for the processing and distribution of three-dimensional biological macromolecular structure data.

Science Business
http://www.sciencebusiness.net/
An independent news service covering how ideas get from lab to market, drawing on a network of leading journalists and scientific institutions, with reports on the first wave of technology, licensing, spin-off investment, contract research, and corporate R&D management.

Science
http://www.sciencemag.org/

Science News Online
http://www.sciencenews.org/
The weekly newsmagazine of science.

Scientific American
http://www.sciam.com/
Current events in science and technology.

U.S. Department of Health and Human Services
http://www.os.dhhs.gov/

World Health Organization
http://www.who.int/en/

Nanotechnology and Microelectromechanical Systems

Ethical Issues in Nanotechnology
http://www.ethicsweb.ca/ nanotechnology/
A starting point for exploring ethical issues related to nanoscience and nanotechnology.

NanoBusiness Alliance
http://nanoenergysummit.org/

A collective voice for the emerging small-tech industry with a range of initiatives to support and strengthen the nanotechnology business community.

Nanoelectronics Planet
http://www.internetnews.com/

Nanotechnology Investment
http://www.nanotechnology investment.com/
A growing list of publicly traded companies in the nanotech sector, as well as industry and stock news, articles, links, research, and resources for interested investors.

Nanotechnology Now
http://www.nanotech-now.com/
A nanotechnology portal with basic news and general information, covering nanospace and reporting on future disruptive sciences such as microelectromechanical systems (MEMS), quantum computing, nanomedicine, and molecular biology.

News.NanoApex
http://www.nanotechnology.com/
Breaking news, exclusive small-tech resources, large knowledge databases, and a place to discuss nanotech and MEMS with a growing community.

Small Times
http://www.smalltimes.com/
Nanotech and microtech news.

Technology and Telecommunications

Bell Labs Networking Research Laboratory
http://www.bell-labs.com/

CNET
http://www.cnet.com/
Technology news, reviews, articles, downloads, and much more.

Commerce Net
http://www.commerce.net/
A business development network for the advancement of e-commerce.

DSL Reports
http://www.dslreports.com/
Find high-speed access in your area.

Evolt
http://www.evolt.org/
Essential articles for all Web developers and designers.

Expresscopy.com
http://www.expresscopy.com/
Low-cost brochures, business cards, and more; same-day printing, with free overnight delivery.

FreeConference.com
http://www.freeconference.com/
Free conference calling, with local conference numbers across the country.

Inform IT
http://www.informit.com/index.aspx
Articles and tutorials for programmers and Web designers.

Insight Research Corporation
http://www.insight-corp.com/
Market research and strategic analysis for the telecom industry.

Intel Microprocessor Research
http://www.intel.com/research/mrl/

Internet World
http://www.internetworld.com/

Internet business news, papers, and blogs, drawing content from sites such as CNET and *Information Week*.

Joel on Software
http://www.joelonsoftware.com/
A large collection of excellent essays on user interface design, growing and managing a top-notch development team, project management, and many other topics.

Microsoft Systems and Networking Research Group
http://research.microsoft.com/sn/

The Motley Fool
http://www.fool.com/index.aspx
Includes computer hardware news.

National Laboratory for Applied Network Research
http://www.nlanr.net/

Netcraft
http://uptime.netcraft.com/up/graph/
Find out which operating system any Web server is running.

Network Solutions Who Is Directory
http://www.networksolutions.com/whois/index.jsp
Find domain owners.

Networking Research at Stanford
http://klamath.stanford.edu/networking/

Oak Ridge National Laboratory High Performance Networking Research
http://www.csm.ornl.gov/newNR.html

Paul Graham
http://www.paulgraham.com/
A collection of sophisticated essays on software development, programming languages, spam, and society.

Slashdot
http://slashdot.org/
News for nerds.

Switchboard
http://www.switchboard.com/
Business and residential phone listings.

Telecommunications Industry Association (TIA)
http://www.tiaonline.org/
TIA represents providers of communications and information technology products and services for the global marketplace through its core competencies in standards development and domestic and international advocacy, as well as market development and trade promotion programs.

Telephony Online
http://telephonyonline.com/
The leading publication for all communications service providers—new and incumbent, wireline and wireless—packed full of news, articles, analysis, white papers, webcasts, and more.

Trace Center Computer Access
http://trace.wisc.edu/world/computer_access/
Links to cooperative efforts by many of the major computer and software developers toward making computers and software more usable for all.

YouSendIt
http://www.yousendit.com/
Free service for transferring files that are too large to send by e-mail.

Arizona

Arizona Angels Investor Network
http://www.arizonaangels.com/index.htm
Arizona Angels, founded in 1999, is a group of accredited investors who

invest primarily in Arizona-based early-stage and developing-growth companies.

Arizona Bioindustry Association
http://www.azbio.org/
A statewide organization that promotes the growth of the bioindustry in the areas of public policy, member services, education, business networking, and entrepreneurial endeavors.

Arizona Business Accelerator (AzBA)
http://www.azba.biz/
AzBA provides business development resources and capital to innovators in Arizona. Services are provided in exchange for warrants or equity, so there is no out-of-pocket cost for its wide array of technical, managerial, and financial services.

Arizona Center for Innovation
http://www.azinnovation.com/
The Arizona Center for Innovation is a new high-tech incubator promoting the development of high-technology companies in southern Arizona through a disciplined program of business development.

Arizona Corporation Commission
http://www.cc.state.az.us/
Resources for getting your business established in Arizona. Use the commission's STARPAS System (http://starpas.azcc.gov/) to look up corporate information about Arizona companies.

Arizona Department of Commerce Small Business Services
http://www.azcommerce.com/BusAsst/SmallBiz/
Small Business Services (SBS) offers support, opportunities, and advocacy through several key functions,

such as what you need to know to start, expand, or relocate a business in Arizona or how to collaborate with state agencies and numerous business organizations to promote entrepreneurship among minority- or woman-owned, small, and disadvantaged business enterprises.

Arizona Entrepreneurship Conference
http://www.grid7.com/archives/59_arizona-entrepreneurship-conference-2006-audio.html
Audio for all sessions of the first annual Arizona Entrepreneurship Conference, held in November 2006, are available from Grid7 as individual MP3 downloads, streaming audio, or a single zip file of all conference audio.

Arizona Internet Professionals Association (AZIPA)
http://www.azipa.org/

Arizona SCORE (Service Corps of Retired Executives)
http://scoreaz.org/index_main.php
SCORE is a resource partner with the U.S. Small Business Administration. Arizona SCORE is dedicated to aiding in the formation, growth, and success of small business in Arizona and nationwide. Its main function is to provide confidential, one-on-one business counseling to meet the needs of business start-up and expansion and to provide problem-solving assistance.

Arizona Small Business Association
http://www.asba.com/
Networking, seminars, health care, and other benefits for small businesses.

Arizona State University Technopolis
http://www.asutechnopolis.org/

Developed to help transform the metro area's knowledge economy.

Arizona Technology Council
http://www.aztechcouncil.com/
Dedicated to advancing the technology industry in Arizona.

Arizona Venture Capital and Angel Fund Directory
http://www.caycon.com/arizona_venture_capital.php
Directory of all known venture funds, angel investor groups, major corporate investors, SBICs, and other related entities based in Arizona. Also includes a few non-Arizona funds that have invested in Arizona companies.

Enterprise Network
http://www.en.org/
The leading entrepreneurial organization in Arizona.

Inventors Association of Arizona (IAA)
http://www.azinventors.org/
The IAA is a nonprofit organization dedicated to helping individual inventors get their products to market.

Invest Southwest Capital Conference
http://www.investsouthwest.org/
One of the best ways for investors to connect with the Southwest's most promising ventures.

KeytLaw
http://www.keytlaw.com/index.html
Directory of articles covering a wide variety of Arizona and federal legal topics.

Northern Arizona Technology and Business Incubator (NATBI)
http://www.natbi.org/

NATBI is a nonprofit small business assistance program designed to help facilitate the growth of new and existing businesses in northern Arizona.

Phoenix Export Assistance Center of the U.S. Department of Commerce
http://www.azexport.com/

Tech Oasis
http://www.techoasis.com/
Monthly networking events and much more.

TiE Arizona
http://az.tie.org/
A nonprofit global network of entrepreneurs and professionals established to foster entrepreneurship and nurture entrepreneurs in Arizona.

Atlanta

Advanced Technology Development Center (ATDC)
http://www.atdc.org/
The ATDC strives to increase the technology business base in Georgia by helping entrepreneurs launch and build successful high-tech companies.

Association for Corporate Growth (ACG), Atlanta Chapter
http://chapters.acg.org/atlanta/
ACG comprises more than 10,000 members from corporations, private equity, finance, and professional service firms representing *Fortune* 500, *Fortune* 1,000, FTSE 100, and midmarket companies in fifty-three chapters in North America and Europe. ACG Atlanta is one of the oldest and most active chapters, with nearly 500 individuals in decision-making positions who have personal and professional interest in corporate growth (including internal development, mergers and acquisitions, joint ventures, licensing arrangements, or the provision of services facilitating such activities).

Atlanta Business Chronicle
http://atlanta.bizjournals.com/atlanta/
Weekly source of latest news in the Metro Atlanta business, political, civic, financial, media, and nonprofit communities.

Atlanta Business School Alliance (ABSA)
http://www.atlantabsa.com/
ABSA comprises Atlanta-area alumni clubs from leading business schools nationally and internationally, working together to offer their members opportunities to network and to learn about and discuss leading-edge business thinking and practices.

Atlanta CEO Council
http://www.atlantaceo.org/
A venue where CEOs from Atlanta's leading companies connect with peers.

Atlanta Venture Forum
http://www.atlantaventureforum.org
Founded in 1984 to foster closer professional relationships among the members of the Southeast private equity community through the exchange of information and ideas, the Atlanta Venture Forum has grown into the largest trade association for private equity investors in the Southeast.

Georgia Research Alliance (GRA)
http://www.gra.org/
Since 1990, GRA has helped recruit world-renowned scientists, called Georgia Research Alliance Eminent Scholars; helped fuel the launch of more than 125 companies; and served as a key catalyst for two dozen centers of research excellence—university-based enterprises that serve as magnets for scientists and federal research dollars.

MIT Enterprise Forum of Atlanta
http://www.mitforumatlanta.org/
The MIT Enterprise Forum of Atlanta
provides educational programs
and services promoting and
strengthening innovation and entrepreneurship at the intersection of
business and technology in the
Southeast.

TechLinks
http://www.techlinks.net
TechLinks is the technology-focused
media company developing business
opportunities for Georgia technology
companies through a vibrant combination of online content, print publications, event media services, and
online Atlanta and Georgia business
directory and technology
marketplaces.

Technology Association of Georgia
(TAG)
http://www.tagonline.org
TAG is dedicated to the promotion
and economic advancement of the
state's technology industry. It provides leadership in driving initiatives in the areas of policy, capital,
education, and giving.

Technology Executive Roundtable
(TER), Atlanta Chapter
http://www.ter-atlanta.com/
TER provides CEOs, CFOs, and general
managers a forum to share, challenge,
and test their ideas through candid
talk about complex issues.

TiE Atlanta
http://www.tie-atlanta.org/
A nonprofit global network of
entrepreneurs and professionals,
established to foster entrepreneurship and nurture entrepreneurs in
Atlanta.

Boston

Angel Healthcare Investors
http://www.hcangels.com/
Boston-based angel investment group
specializing in the health care sector.

Arthur M. Blank Center for Entrepreneurship at Babson College
http://www3.babson.edu/eship/
Great research material and other
resources for entrepreneurs. Babson
College was ranked number one in
entrepreneurship in *U.S. News and
World Report*'s ranking of MBA
programs.

Arthur Rock Center for
Entrepreneurship
http://www.hbs.edu/
entrepreneurship/
Entrepreneurial news, research, and
resources at Harvard Business
School.

Boston Business Journal
http://boston.bizjournals.com/
boston/
Boston area business news.

Boston Entrepreneurs' Network
http://www.boston-enet.org/
The Boston Entrepreneurs' Network
provides the New England inventive
and entrepreneurial community with
the information necessary to transform an abstract idea from concept
into a product or service. The "E-
Net" is a special interest group of
the Boston Section IEEE.

Cambridge Innovation Center
http://www.cambridgeincubator.
com/
More than 100 growing technology
companies in the Boston area are
leveraging the facilities, business,
and technical services at the

Cambridge Innovation Center to succeed and thrive.

Center for Women Entrepreneurs
http://www.cweboston.org/
Programs and services tailored to meet the needs of women starting, growing, or learning how to operate their businesses.

Cherrystone Angel Group
http://cherrystoneangelgroup.com/
Rhode Island-based angel investor group.

Common Angels
http://www.commonangels.com/
Lexington, Massachusetts-based angel investor group, focusing on software.

eCoast Angels
http://ecoastangels.com/
New Hampshire-based angel investor group.

Entrepreneurship at Harvard Business School
http://www.hbs.edu/entrepreneurship/
Great articles, events, and research for entrepreneurs.

Hub Angels Investment Group
http://www.hubangels.com/
Boston-based angel investment group.

Inventors' Association of New England (IANE)
http://www.inventne.org/
IANE is a group of inventors having a common interest in helping fellow inventors get their inventions moving along the right track. Expert speakers and members are available to provide guidance to inventors in the patent protection area, marketing, product development, prototyping, and other topics of interest to inventors.

Launchpad Venture Group
http://www.launchpadventuregroup.com/
Boston-based angel investor group with more than sixty active members with typical investments in the $100,000 to $500,000 range.

Massachusetts Biomedical Initiatives (MBI)
http://www.massbiomed.org/
MBI is a private, nonprofit economic development organization dedicated to job creation throughout Massachusetts by promoting the growth of start-up biomedical companies.

Massachusetts Biotechnology Council
http://www.massbio.org/
The Massachusetts Biotechnology Council is a not-for-profit organization that provides services and support for the Massachusetts biotechnology industry.

MedDev Group (MDG)
http://www.meddevgroup.org/
MDG is a medical device and technology networking organization whose purpose is to enhance business development opportunities for its members.

MIT Enterprise Forum of Cambridge
http://www.mitforumcambridge.org/
The MIT Enterprise Forum of Cambridge is a volunteer, nonprofit organization based at the Massachusetts Institute of Technology. Its mission is to promote and strengthen the process of starting and growing innovative and technology-oriented companies by providing services and programs that educate, inform,

and support the entrepreneurial community.

MIT Entrepreneurship Center
http://entrepreneurship.mit.edu/
The MIT Entrepreneurship Center team provides content, context, and contacts that enable entrepreneurs to design and launch successful new ventures based on innovative technologies.

River Valley Investors
http://www.rivervalleyinvestors.com/
Massachusetts-based angel investor group.

Small Business Administration (SBA)
http://www.sba.gov/localresources/district/ma/index.html
The SBA's Massachusetts district offers access to capital, entrepreneurial development, government contracting, and other information.

TiE Boston
http://www.tie-boston.org/
TiE-Boston is a not-for-profit Boston organization with a mission to foster and support entrepreneurship, either in a start-up context or within a larger company.

Walnut Venture Associates
http://www.walnutventures.com/site3/home.html
Massachusetts-based angel investor group.

Los Angeles

Business Technology Center (BTC) of Los Angeles County
http://www.lacdc.org/cdcwebsite/labtc/home.aspx
The BTC is the largest technology incubator in California, with a mission of

assisting start-up and early stage technology firms grow and prosper.

Fresh News
http://freshnews.com/
California technology news.

Keiretsu Forum
http://www.k4forum.com/chapters/los_angeles/index.html
Los Angeles angel investor group.

L.A. County Technology Week
http://www.latechweek.com/
Hosts high-profile events for technology entrepreneurs in Southern California.

Los Angeles Venture Association
http://www.lava.org/mc/page.do
The Los Angeles Venture Association supports the development of emerging growth and middle-market companies in Southern California by creating an environment to provide access to financial, professional, and technological resources.

Pasadena Angels
http://www.pasadenaangels.com/
Angel investor group in Pasadena, California.

Pasadena Entretec
http://www.pasadenaentretec.com/
Pasadena Entretec is a nonprofit corporation offering access to the financing leads, real estate, people, and partners that will help businesses thrive.

SoCalTech.com
http://www.socaltech.com/
SoCalTech provides breaking news coverage of Southern California tech companies, including venture funding, business news, and interviews

with local technology entrepreneurs and industry luminaries.

Tech Coast Angels
http://www.techcoastangels.com/
Angel investor group in Southern California.

Technology Council of Southern California
http://www.tcosc.org/
Educational events, peer-to-peer executive forums, networking and contacts, access to financing, public relations and promotional opportunities, assistance on critical business issues, training, and an overall sense of community for the Southern California software community.

New York

New York Business Development Corporation (NYBDC)
http://www.nybdc.com/
The NYBDC's mission is to promote economic activity within New York State by providing innovative loans to small and medium-size businesses; to assist banks in making such loans; and, particularly, to assist minority- and woman-owned businesses by offering credit opportunities not otherwise available to them.

Tech Valley Angel Network (TVAN)
http://www.techvalleyangels.com/06index.cfm
TVAN is an angel investor network looking for opportunities in technology-based companies within 150 miles of Albany, New York. It generally prefers companies seeking $1 million or less.

San Diego

BIOCOM
http://www.biocom.org/

California Healthcare Institute
http://www.chi.org/
Advocate for California's biomedical industry.

San Diego MIT Enterprise Forum
http://www.sdmitforum.org/

San Diego Software Industry Council
http://www.sdsic.org/

San Diego Venture Group
http://www.sdvg.org/
A nonprofit business organization whose mission is to provide an informal atmosphere that fosters ideas on how to form, fund, and build new ventures.

San Diego World Trade Center (SDWTC)
http://www.sdwtc.org/
SDWTC is a public-private, nonprofit international trade facilitation organization committed to the development and expansion of international trade and commerce opportunities for the San Diego region. It provides international trade counseling, research, referrals, and leads to companies worldwide, offering matchmaking services to inbound delegations and outbound trade missions.

UCSD Connect
http://www.connect.org/
Fosters entrepreneurship in the San Diego region by catalyzing, accelerating, and supporting the growth of the most promising technology and life science businesses.

Seattle

Northwest Entrepreneur Network
http://www.nwen.org/
The Northwest Entrepreneur Network, a nonprofit organization, is dedicated to helping entrepreneurs succeed.

Activities and programs are focused on building the entrepreneurial and venture community in the Northwest and enabling entrepreneurs to access resources and funding to accelerate their business growth.

Seattle Chapter of the Association for Corporate Growth (ACG)
http://chapters.acg.org/seattle/
Although the ACG is for midsize and large companies, it sponsors events such as the Northwest Growth Financing Conference.

Seattle Post-Intelligencer Venture Capital Notebook
http://seattlepi.nwsource.com/venture/
News source on venture capital and entrepreneurship in the Pacific Northwest region.

San Francisco Bay Area/Silicon Valley

Band of Angels
http://www.bandangels.com/
Angel investor group in the Silicon Valley region.

Bay Area Bioscience Center
http://www.baybio.org/wt/page/index
A public-private partnership and forum organized to strengthen the competitiveness of the Bay Area as the premier global location for bioscience research, education, and industry.

Churchill Club
http://www.churchillclub.org/
Networking and events for Bay Area entrepreneurs and technology visionaries.

Keiretsu Forum
http://www.k4forum.com/chapters/norcal/index.html
Bay area angel investor group.

San Francisco Chronicle
http://www.sfgate.com/chronicle/

San Jose Entrepreneur Center
http://www.ecenteronline.org/

San Jose Mercury News
http://www.mercurynews.com/

Silicon Valley Association of Startup Entrepreneurs (SVASE)
http://www.svase.org/
Founded in 1995 by entrepreneurs for entrepreneurs, SVASE seeks to accelerate the formation, growth, and success of technology-based companies by empowering entrepreneurs. SVASE provides a wealth of resources on its Web site, plus opportunities for learning and networking with potential investors and other entrepreneurs at the twelve to fifteen events it holds each month in the San Francisco Bay area.

Silicon Valley SCORE
http://www.svscore.org/
Seminars and free business consulting for small businesses and start-ups.

Silicon Valley Small Business Development Center
http://www.siliconvalley-sbdc.org/

Silicon Valley Software Technology Association
http://www.svsoftware.org/
The Silicon Valley Software Technology Association is a volunteer-based nonprofit organization, with more than 1,100 members, that promotes technological, professional, and scientific development in the software industry.

SiliconValley.com
http://www.siliconvalley.com/

APPENDIX B: GOOGLE'S S-1 FILING

As filed with the Securities and Exchange Commission on *April 29, 2004*

Registration No. 333-

SECURITIES AND EXCHANGE COMMISSION
Washington, D.C. 20549

FORM S-1
REGISTRATION STATEMENT
Under
The Securities Act of 1933

GOOGLE INC.
(Exact name of Registrant as specified in its charter)

Delaware	7375	77-0493581
(State or other jurisdiction of incorporation or organization)	(Primary Standard Industrial Classification Code Number)	(I.R.S. Employer Identification Number)

1600 Amphitheatre Parkway
Mountain View, CA 94043
(650) 623-4000

(Address, including zip code, and telephone number, including area code, of Registrant's principal executive offices)

Eric Schmidt
Chief Executive Officer
Google Inc.
1600 Amphitheatre Parkway
Mountain View, CA 94043
(650) 623-4000

(Name, address, including zip code, and telephone number, including area code, of agent for service)

Copies to:

Larry W. Sonsini, Esq.	David C. Drummond, Esq.	William H. Hinman, Jr., Esq.
David J. Segre, Esq.	Jeffery L. Donovan, Esq.	Simpson Thacher & Bartlett
Wilson Sonsini Goodrich & Rosati, P.C.	Anna Itoi, Esq.	LLP
650 Page Mill Road	Google Inc.	3330 Hillview Avenue
Palo Alto, California 94304-1050	1600 Amphitheatre Parkway	Palo Alto, California 94304
(650) 493-9300	Mountain View, CA 94043	(650) 251-5000
	(650) 623-4000	

Approximate date of commencement of proposed sale to the public: As soon as practicable after the effective date of this Registration Statement.

If any of the securities being registered on this Form are being offered on a delayed or continuous basis pursuant to Rule 415 under the Securities Act of 1933, as amended (the *"Securities Act"*), check the following box.

If this Form is filed to register additional securities for an offering pursuant to Rule 462(b) under the Securities Act, please check the following box and list the Securities Act registration number of the earlier effective registration statement for the same offering.

If this Form is a post-effective amendment filed pursuant to Rule 462(c) under the Securities Act, check the following box and list the Securities Act registration number of the earlier effective registration statement for the same offering.

If this Form is a post-effective amendment filed pursuant to Rule 462(d) under the Securities Act, check the following box and list the Securities Act registration statement number of the earlier effective registration statement for the same offering.

If delivery of the prospectus is expected to be made pursuant to Rule 434, check the following box. _____

CALCULATION OF REGISTRATION FEE

Title of Each Class of Securities to be Registered	Proposed Maximum Aggregate Offering Price (1)(2)	Amount of Registration Fee
Class A common stock, par value $0.001 per share	$ 2,718,281,828	$ 344,406.31

(1) Estimated solely for the purpose of computing the amount of the registration fee, in accordance with to Rule 457(o) promulgated under the Securities Act of 1933.
(2) Includes offering price of shares that the underwriters have the option to purchase to cover over-allotments, if any.

_____

The Registrant hereby amends this Registration Statement on such date or dates as may be necessary to delay its effective date until *the Registrant* shall file a further amendment which specifically states that this Registration Statement shall thereafter become effective in accordance with Section 8(a) of the Securities Act or until the Registration Statement shall become effective on such date as the Securities and Exchange Commission, acting pursuant to said Section 8(a), may determine.

Table of Contents
The information in this prospectus is not complete and may be changed. We may not sell these securities until the registration statement filed with

the Securities and Exchange Commission is effective. **This prospectus is not an offer to sell these securities and we are not soliciting any offer to buy these securities in any jurisdiction where the offer or sale is not permitted.**

Prospectus (Subject to Completion)

Dated *April 29, 2004*

Shares

Google

Class A Common Stock

—————

Google Inc. is offering shares of Class A common stock and the selling stockholders are offering shares of Class A common stock. We will not receive any proceeds from the sale of shares by the selling stockholders. This is our initial public offering and no public market currently exists for our shares. We anticipate that the initial public offering price will be between $ and $ per share.

—————

Following this offering, we will have two classes of authorized common stock, Class A common stock and Class B common stock. The rights of the holders of Class A common stock and Class B common stock are identical, except with respect to voting and conversion. Each share of Class A common stock is entitled to one vote per share. Each share of Class B common stock is entitled to ten votes per share and is convertible at any time into one share of Class A common stock.

—————

We expect to apply to list our Class A common stock on either the New York Stock Exchange or the Nasdaq National Market under the symbol ".".

—————

Investing in our Class A common stock involves risks. See *"Risk Factors"* beginning on page 4.

	Price to Public	Underwriting Discounts and Commissions	Proceeds to Google	Proceeds to Selling Stockholders
Per Share	$	$	$	$
Total	$	$	$	$

—————

Google has granted the underwriters the right to purchase up to an additional shares to cover over-allotments.

The price to the public and allocation of shares will be determined primarily by an auction process. As part of this auction process, we are attempting to assess the market demand for our Class A common stock and to set the size and price to the public of this offering to meet that demand. Buyers hoping to capture profits shortly after our Class A common stock begins trading may be disappointed. The method for submitting bids and a more detailed description of this process are included in *"Auction Process"* beginning on page 25.

The Securities and Exchange Commission and state securities regulators have not approved or disapproved of these securities, or determined if this prospectus is truthful or complete. Any representation to the contrary is a criminal offense.

It is expected that the shares will be delivered to purchasers on or about, 2004.

Morgan Stanley   **Credit Suisse First Boston**

Table of Contents

TABLE OF CONTENTS

	Page
Letter from the Founders	i
Prospectus Summary	1
The Offering	2
Risk Factors	4
Special Note Regarding Forward-Looking Statements	24
Auction Process	25
Use of Proceeds	31
Dividend Policy	31
Cash and Capitalization	32
Dilution	34
Selected Consolidated Financial Data	35
Management's Discussion and Analysis of Financial Condition and Results of Operations	37
Business	57
Management	69
Certain Relationships and Related Party Transactions	82
Principal and Selling Stockholders	84
Description of Capital Stock	86
Rescission Offer	92
Shares Eligible for Future Sale	93
Underwriters	96
Notice to Canadian Residents	99
Legal Matters	100
Experts	100
Where You Can Find Additional Information	100
Index to Consolidated Financial Statements	F-1

You should rely only on the information contained in this prospectus. We have not authorized anyone to provide you with information that is different from that contained in this prospectus. We are offering to sell, and seeking offers to buy, shares of our Class A common stock only in jurisdictions where offers and sales are permitted. The information in this prospectus is complete and accurate only as of the date of the front cover regardless of the time of delivery of this prospectus or of any sale of shares. Except where the context requires otherwise, in this prospectus, the *"Company," "Google," "we," "us"* and *"our"* refer to Google Inc., a Delaware corporation, and, where appropriate, its subsidiaries.

We have not undertaken any efforts to qualify this offering for offers to individual investors in any jurisdiction outside the U.S.; therefore, individual investors located outside the U.S. should not expect to be eligible to participate in this offering.

Until, 2004, 25 days after the date of this offering, all dealers that effect transactions in our shares, whether or not participating in this offering, may be required to deliver a prospectus. This is in addition to the dealers' obligation to deliver a prospectus when acting as underwriters and with respect to their unsold allotments or subscriptions.

LETTER FROM THE FOUNDERS
"AN OWNER'S MANUAL" FOR GOOGLE'S SHAREHOLDERS[1]

Introduction

Google is not a conventional company. We do not intend to become one. Throughout Google's evolution as a privately held company, we have managed Google differently. We have also emphasized an atmosphere of creativity and challenge, which has helped us provide unbiased, accurate and free access to information for those who rely on us around the world.

Now the time has come for the company to move to public ownership. This change will bring important benefits for our employees, for our present and future shareholders, for our customers, and most of all for Google users. But the standard structure of public ownership may jeopardize the independence and focused objectivity that have been most important in Google's past success and that we consider most fundamental for its future. Therefore, we have designed a corporate structure that will protect Google's ability to innovate and retain its most distinctive characteristics. We are confident that, in the long run, this will bring Google and its shareholders, old and new, the greatest economic returns. We want to clearly explain our plans and the reasoning and values behind them. We are delighted you are considering an investment in Google and are reading this letter.

Sergey and I intend to write you a letter like this one every year in our annual report. We'll take turns writing the letter so you'll hear directly from each of us. We ask that you read this letter in conjunction with the rest of this prospectus.

Serving End Users

Sergey and I founded Google because we believed we could provide a great service to the world—instantly delivering relevant information on any topic. Serving our end users is at the heart of what we do and remains our number one priority.

Our goal is to develop services that improve the lives of as many people as possible—to do things that matter. We make our services as widely available as we can by supporting over 97 languages and by providing most services for free. Advertising is our principal source of revenue, and the ads we provide are relevant and useful rather than intrusive and annoying. We strive to provide users with great commercial information.

We are proud of the products we have built, and we hope that those we create in the future will have an even greater positive impact on the world.

Long Term Focus

As a private company, we have concentrated on the long term, and this has served us well. As a public company, we will do the same. In our opinion, outside pressures too often tempt companies to sacrifice long-term opportunities to meet quarterly market expectations. Sometimes this pressure has caused companies to manipulate financial results in order to "make their quarter." In Warren Buffett's words, "We won't 'smooth' quarterly or annual results: If earnings figures are lumpy when they reach headquarters, they will be lumpy when they reach you."

If opportunities arise that might cause us to sacrifice short term results but are in the best long term interest of our shareholders, *we will take those opportunities*. We will have the fortitude to do this. We would request that our shareholders take the long term view.

Many companies are under pressure to keep their earnings in line with analysts' forecasts. Therefore, they often accept smaller, but predictable, earnings rather than larger and more unpredictable returns. Sergey and I feel this is harmful, and we intend to steer in the opposite direction.

Google has had adequate cash to fund our business and has generated additional cash through operations. This gives us the flexibility to weather costs, benefit from opportunities and optimize our long term earnings. For example, in our ads system we make many improvements that affect revenue in both directions. These are in areas like end user relevance and satisfaction, advertiser satisfaction, partner needs and targeting technology. We release improvements immediately rather than delaying them, even though delay might give *"smoother"* financial results. You have our commitment to execute quickly to achieve long term value rather than making the quarters more predictable.

We will make decisions on the business fundamentals, not accounting considerations, and always with the long term welfare of our company and shareholders in mind.

Although we may discuss long term trends in our business, we do not plan to give earnings guidance in the traditional sense. We are not able to predict our business within a narrow range for each quarter. We recognize that our duty is to advance our shareholders' interests, and we believe that artificially creating short term target numbers serves our shareholders poorly. We would prefer not to be asked to make such predictions, and if asked we will respectfully decline. A management team distracted by a series of short term targets is as pointless as a dieter stepping on a scale every half hour.

Risk vs Reward in the Long Run

Our business environment changes rapidly and needs long term investment. We will not hesitate to place major bets on promising new opportunities.

We will not shy away from high-risk, high-reward projects because of short term earnings pressure. Some of our past bets have gone extraordinarily well, and others have not. Because we recognize the pursuit of such projects as the key to our long term success, we will continue to seek them out. For example, we would fund projects that have a 10% chance of earning a billion dollars over the long term. Do not be surprised if we place smaller bets in areas that seem very speculative or even strange. As the ratio of reward to risk increases, we will accept projects further outside our normal areas, especially when the initial investment is small.

We encourage our employees, in addition to their regular projects, to spend 20% of their time working on what they think will most benefit Google. This empowers them to be more creative and innovative. Many of our significant advances have happened in this manner. For example, AdSense for content and Google News were both prototyped in "20% time". Most risky projects fizzle, often teaching us something. Others succeed and become attractive businesses.

We may have quarter-to-quarter volatility as we realize losses on some new projects and gains on others. If we accept this, we can all maximize value in the long term. Even though we are excited about risky projects, we expect to devote the vast majority of our resources to our main businesses, especially since most people naturally gravitate toward incremental improvements.

Executive Roles

We run Google as a triumvirate. Sergey and I have worked closely together for the last eight years, five at Google. Eric, our CEO, joined Google three years ago. The three of us run the company collaboratively with Sergey and me as Presidents. The structure is unconventional, but we have worked successfully in this way.

To facilitate timely decisions, Eric, Sergey and I meet daily to update each other on the business and to focus our collaborative thinking on the most important and immediate issues. Decisions are often made by one of us, with the others being briefed later. This works because we have tremendous trust and respect for each other and we generally think alike. Because of our intense long term working relationship, we can often predict differences of opinion among the three of us. We know that when we disagree, the correct decision is far from obvious. For important decisions, we discuss the issue with the larger team. Eric, Sergey and I run the company without any significant internal conflict, but with healthy debate. As different topics come up, we often delegate decision-making responsibility to one of us.

We hired Eric as a more experienced complement to Sergey and me to help us run the business. Eric was CTO of Sun Microsystems. He was also CEO of Novell and has a Ph.D. in computer science, a very unusual and important combination for Google given our scientific and technical culture. This partnership among the three of us has worked very well and we expect it to continue. The shared judgments and extra energy available from all three of us has significantly benefited Google.

Eric has the legal responsibilities of the CEO and focuses on management of our vice presidents and the sales organization. Sergey focuses on engineering and business deals. I focus on engineering and product management. All three of us devote considerable time to overall management of the company and other fluctuating needs. We are extremely fortunate to have talented management that has grown the company to where it is today—they operate the company and deserve the credit.

Corporate Structure

We are creating a corporate structure that is designed for stability over long time horizons. By investing in Google, you are placing an unusual long-term bet on the team, especially Sergey and me, and on our innovative approach.

We want Google to become an important and significant institution. That takes time, stability and independence. We bridge the media and technology industries, both of which have experienced considerable consolidation and attempted hostile takeovers.

In the transition to public ownership, we have set up a corporate structure that will make it harder for outside parties to take over or influence Google. This structure will also make it easier for our management team to follow the long term, innovative approach emphasized earlier. This structure, called a dual class voting structure, is described elsewhere in this prospectus.

The main effect of this structure is likely to leave our team, especially Sergey and me, with significant control over the company's decisions and fate, as Google shares change hands. New investors will fully share in Google's long term growth but will have less influence over its strategic decisions than they would at most public companies.

While this structure is unusual for technology companies, it is common in the media business and has had a profound importance there. The New York Times Company, the Washington Post Company and Dow Jones, the publisher of *The Wall Street Journal*, all have similar dual class ownership structures. Media observers frequently point out that dual class ownership has allowed these companies to concentrate on their core, long-term interest in serious news coverage, despite fluctuations in quarterly results. The Berkshire Hathaway company has applied the same structure, with similar beneficial effects. From the point of view of long-term success in advancing a company's core values, the structure has clearly been an advantage.

Academic studies have shown that from a purely economic point of view, dual class structures have not harmed the share price of companies. The shares of each of our classes have identical economic rights and differ only as to voting rights.

Google has prospered as a private company. As a public company, we believe a dual class voting structure will enable us to retain many of the positive aspects of being private. We understand some investors do not favor dual class structures. We have considered this point of view carefully, and we have not made our decision lightly. We are convinced that everyone associated with Google—including new investors—will benefit from this structure.

To help us govern, we have recently expanded our Board of Directors to include three additional members. John Hennessy is the President of Stanford and has a Doctoral degree in computer science. Art Levinson is CEO of Genentech and has a Ph.D. in biochemistry. Paul Otellini is President and COO of Intel. We could not be more excited about the caliber and experience of these directors.

We have a world class management team impassioned by Google's mission and responsible for Google's success. We believe the stability afforded by the dual-class structure will enable us to retain our unique culture and continue to attract and retain talented people who are Google's life blood. Our colleagues will be able to trust that they themselves and their labors of hard work, love and creativity will be well cared for by a company focused on stability and the long term.

As an investor, you are placing a potentially risky long term bet on the team, especially Sergey and me. The two of us, Eric and the rest of the management team recognize that our individual and collective interests are deeply aligned with those of the new investors who choose to support Google. Sergey and I are committed to Google for the long term. The broader Google team has also demonstrated an extraordinary commitment to our long term success. With continued hard work and good fortune, this commitment will last and flourish.

When Sergey and I founded Google, we hoped, but did not expect, it would reach its current size and influence. Our intense and enduring interest was to objectively help people find information efficiently. We also believed that searching and organizing all the world's information was an unusually important task that should be carried out by a company that is trustworthy and interested in the public good. We believe a well functioning society should have abundant, free and unbiased access to high quality information. Google therefore has a responsibility to the world. The dual-class structure helps ensure that this responsibility is met. We believe that fulfilling this responsibility will deliver increased value to our shareholders.

Becoming a Public Company

Google should go public soon.

We assumed when founding Google that if things went well, we would likely go public someday. But we were always open to staying private, and a number of developments reduced the pressure to change. We soon were generating cash, removing one important reason why many companies go public. Requirements for public companies became more significant in the wake of recent corporate scandals and the resulting passage of the Sarbanes-Oxley Act. We made business progress we were happy with. Our investors were patient and willing to stay with Google. We have been able to meet our business needs with our current level of cash.

A number of factors weighed on the other side of the debate. Our growth has reduced some of the advantages of private ownership. By law, certain private companies must report as if they were public companies. The deadline imposed by this requirement accelerated our decision. As a smaller private company, Google kept business information closely held, and we believe this helped us against competitors. But, as we grow larger, information becomes more widely known. As a public company, we will of course provide you with all information required by law, and we will also do our best to explain our actions. But we will not unnecessarily disclose all of our strengths, strategies and intentions. We have transferred significant ownership of Google to employees in return for their efforts in building the business. And, we benefited greatly by selling $26 million of stock to our early investors before we were profitable. Thus, employee and investor liquidity were significant factors.

We have demonstrated a proven business model and have designed a corporate structure that will make it easier to become a public company. A large, diverse, enthusiastic shareholder base will strengthen the company and benefit from our continued success. A larger cash balance will provide Google with flexibility and protection against adversity. All in all, going public now is the right decision.

IPO Pricing and Allocation

Informed investors willing to pay the IPO price should be able to buy as many shares as they want, within reason, in the IPO, as on the stock market.

It is important to us to have a fair process for our IPO that is inclusive of both small and large investors. It is also crucial that we achieve a good outcome for Google and its current shareholders. This has led us to pursue an auction-based IPO for our entire offering. Our goal is to have a share price that reflects a fair market valuation of Google and that moves rationally based on changes in our business and the stock market. (The auction process is discussed in more detail elsewhere in this prospectus.)

Many companies have suffered from unreasonable speculation, small initial share float, and boom-bust cycles that hurt them and their investors in the long run. We believe that an auction-based IPO will minimize these problems.

An auction is an unusual process for an IPO in the United States. Our experience with auction-based advertising systems has been surprisingly helpful in the auction design process for the IPO. As in the stock market, if people try to buy more stock than is available, the price will go up. And of course, the price will go down if there aren't enough buyers. This is a simplification, but it captures the basic issues. Our goal is to have an efficient market price—a rational price set by informed buyers and sellers—for our shares at the IPO and afterward. Our goal is to achieve a relatively stable price in the days following the IPO and that buyers and sellers receive a fair price at the IPO.

We are working to create a sufficient supply of shares to meet investor demand at IPO time and after. We are encouraging current shareholders to consider selling some of their shares as part of the offering. These shares will supplement the shares the company sells to provide more supply for investors and hopefully provide a more stable fair price. Sergey and I, among others, are currently planning to sell a fraction of our shares in the IPO. The more shares current shareholders sell, the more likely it is that they believe the price is not unfairly low. The supply of shares available will likely have an effect on the clearing price of the auction. Since the number of shares being sold is likely to be larger at a high price and smaller at a lower price, investors will likely want to consider the scope of current shareholder participation in the IPO. We may communicate from time to time that we would be sellers rather than buyers.

We would like you to invest for the long term, and to do so only at or below what you determine to be a fair price. We encourage investors not to invest in Google at IPO or for some time after, if they believe the price is not sustainable over the long term.

We intend to take steps to help ensure shareholders are well informed. We encourage you to read this prospectus. We think that short term speculation without paying attention to price is likely to lose you money, especially with our auction structure.

Googlers

Our employees, who have named themselves Googlers, are everything. Google is organized around the ability to attract and leverage the talent of exceptional technologists and business people. We have been lucky to recruit many creative, principled and hard working stars. We hope to recruit many more in the future. We will reward and treat them well.

We provide many unusual benefits for our employees, including meals free of charge, doctors and washing machines. We are careful to consider the long term advantages to the company of these benefits. Expect us to add benefits rather than pare them down over time. We believe it is easy to be penny wise and pound foolish with respect to benefits that can save employees considerable time and improve their health and productivity.

The significant employee ownership of Google has made us what we are today. Because of our employee talent, Google is doing exciting work in nearly every area of computer science. We are in a very competitive industry where the quality of our product is paramount. Talented people are attracted to Google because we empower them to change the world; Google has large computational resources and distribution that enables individuals to make a difference. Our main benefit is a workplace with important projects, where employees can contribute and grow. We are focused on providing an environment where talented, hard working people are rewarded for their contributions to Google and for making the world a better place.

Don't be Evil

Don't be evil. We believe strongly that in the long term, we will be better served—as shareholders and in all other ways—by a company that does good things for the world even if we forgo some short term gains. This is an important aspect of our culture and is broadly shared within the company.

Google users trust our systems to help them with important decisions: medical, financial and many others. Our search results are the best we know how to produce. They are unbiased and objective, and we do not accept payment for them or for inclusion or more frequent updating. We also display advertising, which we work hard to make relevant, and we label it clearly. This is similar to a newspaper, where the advertisements are clear and the articles are not influenced by the advertisers' payments. We believe it is important for everyone to have access to the best information and research, not only to the information people pay for you to see.

Making the World a Better Place

We aspire to make Google an institution that makes the world a better place. With our products, Google connects people and information all around the world for free. We are adding other powerful services such as Gmail that provides an efficient one gigabyte Gmail account for free. By releasing services for free, we hope to help bridge the digital divide. AdWords connects users and advertisers efficiently, helping both. AdSense helps fund a huge variety of online web sites and enables authors who could not otherwise publish. Last year we created Google Grants—a growing program in which hundreds of non-profits addressing issues, including the environment, poverty and human rights, receive free advertising. And now, we are in the process of establishing the Google Foundation. We intend to contribute significant resources to the foundation, including employee time and approximately 1% of Google's equity and profits in some form. We hope someday this institution may eclipse Google itself in terms of overall world impact by ambitiously applying innovation and significant resources to the largest of the world's problems.

Summary and Conclusion

Google is not a conventional company. Eric, Sergey and I intend to operate Google differently, applying the values it has developed as a private company to its future as a public company. Our mission and business description are available in the rest of the prospectus; we encourage you to carefully read this information. We will optimize for the long term rather than trying to produce smooth earnings for each quarter. We will support selected high-risk, high-reward projects and manage our portfolio of projects. We will run the company collaboratively with Eric, our CEO, as a team of three. We are conscious of our duty as fiduciaries for our shareholders, and we will fulfill those responsibilities. We will continue to attract creative, committed new employees, and we will welcome support from new shareholders. We will live up to our *"don't be evil"* principle by keeping user trust and not accepting payment for search results. We have a dual-class structure that is biased toward stability and independence and that requires investors to bet on the team, especially Sergey and me.

In this letter we have explained our thinking on why Google is better off going public. We have talked about our IPO auction method and our desire for stability and access for all investors. We have discussed our goal to have investors who determine a rational price and invest for the long term only if they can buy at that price. Finally, we have discussed our desire to create an ideal working environment that will ultimately drive the success of Google by retaining and attracting talented Googlers.

We have tried hard to anticipate your questions. It will be difficult for us to respond to them given legal constraints during our offering process. We look forward to a long and hopefully prosperous relationship with you, our new investors. We wrote this letter to help you understand our company.

We have a strong commitment to our users worldwide, their communities, the web sites in our network, our advertisers, our investors, and of course our employees. Sergey and I, and the team will do our best to make Google a long term success and the world a better place.

Larry Page   Sergey Brin

Index

Acquisitions, 98–102; strategy to use, 102; success strategy, 100–102

Advanced Technology Development Center, 48

"Adventure capitalists," 45

Alternative capital, avenues for, 74–81

Angel investors, 45–47

Association for Corporate Growth (ACG), 118

Astute investors, 3

Bench strength, 9–10; critical areas, 10

Big guns, institutional investors, 50–73

BlackBerry, 1, 59

Bock, Larry, 8, 17, 46

BRIC countries, 91

Bridge loans, 34

Broken processes, 41

Business and taking capital, 41

Business incubators, 47–48

Business plan writing, 114; advantages and disadvantages, 115; four basic approaches to preparing a business plan, 115–17; full-blown, 129; half-baked, 129

Capital infusion, anticipated, 27

Capital-raising process, 128

CAP table, 20

Cash-flow rates, 96

Challenge Fund Program for Technology Development, 53

Chasm, 5–7; crossing the, 5; technology adoption life cycle, 6

Chevron Technologies Ventures, 59

Chipotle Mexican Grill, 3

Chrysler Credit, 71

Chrysler Design Award, 34

Client–intermediary relationships, 123

Coca-Cola Company, 60

Collins, Jim, 19

Columbus, Christopher, 53

Company's distribution channel, 51

Contingency arrangements, 119

Copyright licensing agreements, 79

Corporate sponsors, securing, 80

Corporate venture capital (CVC), 58–61

Creative capital, bootstrapping and early-stage, 33–48

Credible financial statements, 35

Current financial partnership, 112

Deal flow, 66

Diligence support, 114

Dilution, 20

Discounted cash flow (DCF) valuation, 96–97; key questions to determine, 97

Down round, 20

Dumb capital, 16–17

Dumb money pool, keeping yourself out of, 17–19

Earnings per share (EPS), 72

eBay, 11

Ells, Steve, 3
Equipment Leasing Association
  (ELA), 74
Equity financing, 113
Exit strategies, 103–10; how to exit,
  105–8; selecting your, 107–8; when
  to exit, 108–10; why to exit, 104–5
Exit time frame, selecting your,
  109–10
Experts speak, 125–36
"Eyeballs," 96

Factoring, 75–77; advantages of, 76;
  drawbacks of, 76–77
Federal Acquisition Requirement
  (FAR), 54
Financial intermediaries: critical
  success factors, 121–22; processes,
  114; value-added, 112–23
Financial stewardship, 26
Flawed assumptions, 30
Foreign direct investment (FDI), 79
Foreign exchanges, listing on, 91–93
Funding sources, 114
Fundraising: professionals, 112–20;
  timing, amount, and sources of, 8;
  without an objective self-analysis,
  126–27
Fundraising campaign, 130–32

Gartner Hype Cycle, 62; sample for
  emerging technologies, 63
Generic Bank, 37
Generic Corporation, sample term
  sheet, 37–41
Georgian Bank, economic
  conditions, 4
Gerber, Michael, 1
Goedhart, Marc, 96
Going public, 82–88; NASDAQ
  exchange, 82
Good partners, to fuel your growth,
  43
Googlers, 178–79
Google's S-1 filing, first page of, 86
Gordon, Rusty, 4, 6
Government funding, 53–58
Greener pastures, 20–22

Hertz Corporation, 69
Hiring consultants, considerations in,
  119–20
Hitachi Corporate Venture Catalyst
  Division, 59
Home Depot sponsors, NASCAR
  team, 79

Ideal buyer profile (IBP), 7
Ideal customer profile (ICP), 7
Illinois Recycling Grant Program, 53
Incubation programs, 47
Incubator's management, 47
Industry dysfunctions, 41
Industry nuances, 3–4; unique
  approaches, 4
Inflated balance sheet, 9
Initial Public Offering (IPO), 51, 68,
  82–88; disadvantages, 88; trading
  begin, 87; 12-month countdown
  timeline, 83; pricing and allocation,
  177–78; process, 83–85; team, 83–85,
  99; trading, 88
Institutional investors, 50–73; capital
  investors, 51; look for, 50–53
Intel Capital Fund, 58–59
Intellectual Property Owner, 79
Intellectual Property Owners Associa-
  tion, 34
Interested investor, 70
Internal rate of return (IRR), 9–10
International capital, 79
International Organization of
  Securities Commissions (IOSCO),
  92
Investor due-diligence requests,
  122–23
Investment elasticity, sufficient inter-
  est and deep enough pockets for
  future rounds, 8–9

Kawasaki, Guy, 1
Kleiner Perkins iFund, 26
Knox, Tim, 44
Kodak Venture Relations, 59
Kohlberg Kravis Roberts (KKR), 69
Koller, Tim, 96
Krensavage, Cate Cavanagh, 7, 66

Labor-intensive industries, 77
Leasing, 74–75
Lemelson-MIT Awards, 34
Leveraged buyouts (LBO), 69
Licensing, 78–79
Limited liability corporation (LLC), 107
Limited partner (LP), 20, 68
Liquid cash, 33
Litmus test, 120–22
Lux Capital, 8, 17, 46

Management bench strength, 9–10
Market validation, 41–42
Metro-Goldwyn-Mayer (MGM), 69
Misunderstanding value creation, 134
Moore, Geoffrey, 5; technology adoption life cycle, 6
Motorola Ventures, 59
Moving target, 128

NASCAR team, 79
NASDAQ exchange, 82, 85
National Association of Securities Dealers regulations, 119
National Business Incubations Association, 48
National Institutes of Health (NIH), 54
National Science Foundation (NSF), 54; sample program solicitation, 55
National Venture Capital Association, 59
New York Stock Exchange, 90
Nokia Growth Partners, 59
North Carolina's Division of Pollution Prevention and Environmental Assistance, 53

Ogburn, Adam, 4
Overestimating cost savings, 135–36

Palo Alto Capital Partners, 7
Panasonic Digital Concepts Center, 59
"Patient capital," 42
Pellegrino, Michael, 98
PepsiCo, 60
Peters, Alec, 11, 21
Poor cash-flow management, 135

Poor packaging, 130
Postmoney valuation, 10
Premoney valuation, 10
PricewaterhouseCoopers (PwC) survey, 98, 100
Private equity, 67–73; activity, 70; Bahrain-based Islamic Bank, 69; contribution to the global economy, 72–73; Council, 70; firms look for when investing, 71; intelligence, 72; international top 10 global firm, 70; investors look for, 72; myths and misconceptions, 70–71; typical structure, 68
Private equity group (PEG), 9, 68
Profit-to-earnings (PE) ratio, 72
"Program solicitation," 54
Proof of concept (POC), 54
The public market, access to, 82

Raising capital, 2, 30, 50; art of, 120–23; five focus points, 127; for the right reasons, 42; ten-point checklist, 92–93; to become a diversion, 126; when you're in trouble, 127
Reichert, Bill, 121
Relative valuation, 97–98; six factors, 98
Research in motion (RIM), 59
Return on investment (ROI), 81
Reverse mergers, 88–90; capital infusions, 88
Richardson, Clint, 45
"Rocket boosters," 15
Rounds of financing, 20
Royalties and licensing, 77–78
Royalty financing, 77; advantages, 77–78; potential drawbacks, 78

Sample Term Sheet, 37
The Sarbanes-Oxley Act, 51, 82
Savvy entrepreneur, 27, 41, 43, 104
Savvy investors, 3, 16
Scalability challenges, 19
Scalability plan, 18
Schnabl, André, 9
ScreamingSports.com, 11

Securities and exchange commission
(SEC), 52, 84; early interest, 85; first
page of google's s-1 filing, 86, 168;
registration and the prospectus,
84–85
Securities lawyer, 134
Seed capital: bootstrapping to get you
there, 33–41, 50; friends and family
as sources of, 45
Selling securities online, 126
Senior secured credit facility,
37–41
Service Corps of Retired Executives
(SCORE), 118
Short-term borrowing vehicles, 34
Siemens Venture Capital, 59
Significant selling, general, and
administrative (SG&A), 51
Small Business Administration (SBA),
34, 118; loan program, 36;
website, 35
Small Business Development Centers
(SBDCs), 118
Small Business Innovation Research
(SBIR), 53, 55–58
The Small Business Seed Fund for
Technical Innovations, 53
Small Business Technology Transfer
(STTR), 53, 55–58
Smart capital, 14–15, 20
Smart investors and buyers, 106
Software-as-a-service (SaaS) company,
4, 6
Sponsorships, 79–81
Stock exchangers, top six, 91
Strategic Enterprise Fund, 58
Strategic financial planning, 23–25;
astuteness, 29; best practices for
successful, 31; desired output, 27;
entrepreneurs fail to plan, 29–30;
expected input, 26
Strategic investors, 58–60; dealing
with, 60–62; is it right for your
business?, 61

Technology licensing agreements, 79
Tier-one investors, 18
T-Mobile Venture Fund, 59

Trademark licensing or franchising
agreements, 79
Traditional financial planning, 25;
forecasting, 24
Traditional five-year financial models,
alternative, 25–28
Trustworthy investors, 17
Turnaround management association
(TMA), 118

Ultimate Resource Library, 125–26,
137–82; Arizona, 160–62; Atlanta,
162–63; Boston, 163–65; business
planning and research, 142–49;
financial and operational stewardship, 152–54; general science,
155–58; how to get funded, 138–39;
legal insights, 154–55; loans and
grants, 140–41; Los Angeles, 165–66;
marketing best practices, 150–52;
nanotechnology and microelectromechanical systems, 158; New York,
166; San Diego, 166; San Francisco
Bay Area/Silicon Valley, 167; Seattle, 166–67; technology and telecommunications, 158–60; venture capital
resources, 141–42; where to find
angels, 139–40
Undercapitalized companies: beyond
the chasm, 5–7; building wealth,
1–2; industry nuances, 3–4; investment elasticity, 8–9; management
bench strength, 9–10; raising capital,
2; undercapitalized frugalness,
11–13; weathering broader economic
conditions, 4–5; when to start and
from where to take the money, 7–8
Undercapitalized frugalness, 11–13
U.S.–based mobile technology, 79
U.S. GAAP (Generally Accepted
Accounting Principles), 92
U.S. Federal Law, 51

Valuations, 96
Value-added financial intermediaries,
112–23
Value-creation-based performance
metrics, 96

Venture capital community, 45
Venture capitalist (VC), 21, 62–67,
    126, 133; community, 62; funding,
    65; investments, 65; investors, 62,
    67; in your business, 66; start-up
    cycle, 64
"Vesting schedule," 106

Wessels, David, 96
When to exit, 108–10
Why to exit, 104–5
Wild west, 128
Worth of a company, 95–98
Wrong investors, 129
Wrong venture capital firm, 133–34

About the Author

DAVID NOUR is a social networking strategist and one of the foremost thought leaders on the quantifiable value of business relationships. In a global economy that is becoming increasingly disconnected, the Nour Group, Inc., is solving client challenges with intracompany as well as externally focused Strategic Relationship Planning—the process of transforming valuable business relationships into execution, performance, and results.

A native of Iran, David came to the United States with a suitcase, $100, limited family ties, and no fluency in English! Fast-forward twenty-five years, and he has built an impressive career of entrepreneurial success, both within large corporations and early stage ventures.

David is the author of *Relationship Economics* (2008), a senior management advisor, and a featured speaker for corporate, association, and academic forums, where he shares his knowledge and experience as a leading change agent and visionary for Relationship Economics, the art and science of business relationships.

In addition to serving his community as a former board member of the Center for Puppetry Arts and a former cochair of the United Way Tech Initiative, the Bridge, and High Tech Ministries, David is also an active member of several professional organizations, including the Association for Corporate Growth, American Management Association, Institute of Management Consultants, and Society of International Business Fellows.

In recent years, David was named to *Georgia Trend*'s "40 Under 40," the *Atlanta Business Chronicle*'s "Up and Coming," and *Who's Who in Atlanta Technology Awards*. He has been featured in a variety of publications, including the *Wall Street Journal*, the *New York Times*, the *Atlanta Journal and Constitution*, the *Atlanta Business Chronicle*, *SmartMoney.com*, *Forbes Small Business*, *Georgia Trend*, *Entrepreneur*, and *Success*.

David earned an executive MBA from the Goizueta Business School at Emory University, where he often guest lectures, and a BA degree in management from Georgia State University. He currently resides with his family in Atlanta. To learn more about David, visit www.relationshipeconomics. NET.